Two O'Clock Creek

Poems New and Selected

Also by Bruce Hunter

In the Bear's House, novel, 2009
Coming Home From Home, poetry, 2000
Country Music Country, stories, 1996
The Beekeeper's Daughter, poetry, 1986
Benchmark, poetry, 1982
Selected Canadian Rifles, poetry, 1981

Two O'Clock Creek

Poems New and Selected

by
Bruce Hunter

OOLICHAN BOOKS
FERNIE, BRITISH COLUMBIA, CANADA
2010

Copyright © 2010 by Bruce Hunter ALL RIGHTS RESERVED. No part of this publication may be reproduced, stored in a retrieval system, or transmitted, in any form or by any means, without prior written permission of the publisher, except by a reviewer who may quote brief passages in a review to be printed in a newspaper or magazine or broadcast on radio or television; or, in the case of photocopying or other reprographic copying, a licence from ACCESS COPYRIGHT, 6 Adelaide Street East, Suite 900, Toronto, Ontario M5C 1H6.

Library and Archives Canada Cataloguing in Publication

Hunter, Bruce, 1952-

    Two o'clock creek : poems new and selected / by Bruce Hunter.

ISBN 978-0-88982-266-5

    I. Title.

PS8565.U578T86 2010   C811'.54   C2010-905706-6

We gratefully acknowledge the financial support of the Canada Council for the Arts, the British Columbia Arts Council through the BC Ministry of Tourism, Culture, and the Arts, and the Government of Canada through the Book Publishing Industry Development Program, for our publishing activities.

Published by
Oolichan Books
P.O. Box 2278
Fernie, British Columbia
Canada V0B 1M0

www.oolichan.com

Printed in Canada on 100% post consumer recycled FSC-certified paper.

Thank you to Tom Lewis for the cover image of Two O'Clock Falls, AB.

This one's for Lisa.

CONTENTS

Benchmark

For My Brother Daniel / 13
Strong Women / 15
Concrete Visions of Child / 18
Images of War / 19
Savage Stones / 20
Christmas, 1959 / 22
Light Against Light / 24
When Love Was a Fist / 26
The Beekeeper's Daughter / 28
But The Wind / 30
Palamino Prairie, Rattlesnake Summer / 31
January 1966 - Snowshoeing Into Paradise Valley / 33
June 23, 1973 / 35
Towards A Definition of Pornography / 40
Idiot Leaves / 42
Rage / 45
Pony Chase / 47
And I Lay Down in a Field of Wheat / 49
Skyhooks / 51
The Timekeeping Ghosts / 53

The Thorn Garden

Charlie's Poem / 57
Tall Talk / 58
Icon in Rye / 59
Diesel Haiku (Occidental) / 60
Snowplow Driver's Dream / 61

Billy No Longer the Kid / 62
Song for the Quarrymen / 63
Deep in the South of My Country / 65
Spring Opening—Lock Four / 67
The Mower Man / 69
The Thorn Garden / 71
The Worm / 73
Between the Old and the Knowing / 75
Found on a Sundial Dated April 14, 1936 / 76
What the Dead Dream / 77
Hawk on a Shrouded Urn / 79
The Roses / 81
The Scale / 83
The Groundhog's Curse / 86
The Funeral / 87
The Young Widow / 89
Baseball of the Bizarre / 91
Ten Thousand Jaws / 93
Magnolia Fraseri Walt / 94
They Dream of Being Gardeners / 95
Warlock's Arsenal / 97
Selected Canadian Rifles / 100
Meditation on the Improbable History of a Small Town / 104
The Day We Tore Up Stanley's Lawn / 106

Seasons of the City

My Street / 111
Seasons of the City / 113
December Arson in Cabbagetown *(for Andrew Wreggett)* / 115
Near St. Jamestown Cemetery / 117
The Bride of Bay / 118
What I Know About Gerald / 121
What My Students Teach Me / 123

Letters Home

It's Been Said / 129
Lilacs / 131
Picking Apples / 133
Why the Fields Lie Fallow / 134
Letters Home / 136
Tidal Bells / 138
Neruda in the Kitchen / 139
Slow Train Home / 141
Light Over Morning / 143
Preparations / 145
The Ones Without Lovers / 147
Sardinia *(as told by Margaret)* / 149
Manta Ray / 151
When We Were Lovers / 153
Death of the Black Cat / 155

Coming Home From Home

John/John / 163
Sources / 168
The Scottish Grandmothers / 169
The Night You Died / 171
Chasing The Train / 173
The Tomb at Dunn / 174
Homewords / 179
Coming Home From Home / 183
Two O'Clock Creek / 187
Recurring Dreams on a Garden / 190
The Last Days of Klein / 192
Eden on Flamingo / 193

BENCHMARK

FOR MY BROTHER DANIEL

"Benchmark"

starting point of a survey

driving down from survey school
on highway 41 north of Battle River
miles of uninterrupted bush
save one small graveyard
with its white framed mission
beside it tombstones
high-centered in sweetgrass
these final shapes of ancestry
dust and bones without light
faces in the family album
funeral wreaths of ox-eyed daisy
and yarrow mark their roads

"Surveyor"

an explorer, one who determines size
shapes, ownership, and boundaries

or as legitimate history might have you believe
oldest of seven children, my sister tells me
years later, as my mother told only her
there was one other born before all this
before the legal marriage
my mother held him long enough
to name him Daniel
she was told only that
the couple was from Edmonton

is he alive/well my bastard brother
an engineer or a hockey player
some hero in a country song
oblivious to a brother
more surveyor than poet
who drives these roads searching
for the shapes of the ancestor we share

i met a man today
from Edmonton, my height
with the same crooked teeth
dark laugh and eyes caustic
he too was a surveyor.

STRONG WOMEN

in this family
the men are romancers
of whiskey and lies
the drinking tales that have us
leaving Scotland for stealing sheep
Ireland as potato thieves
what is not said
is because of the women
we are men
strong men
any men at all
this poem is for the women

Auntie, a name with the irony
that a big man is named Tiny,
riding west from New Brunswick
by wagon before the railway
in response to a newspaper advertisement:
Wife Wanted
reply Hiram G. Worden Esq.

she came with muslin bags
of shinplasters, gold pieces
a trunkful of whalebone hoop skirts
a sidesaddle, Colt revolver
just in case, and savvy
the latter two of which
she would use some years later
on a burglar entering her bedroom window
comforting him while police arrived
that the bullseye in her mind

was the top button of his shirt
never missed yet wouldn't now

Hiram G. came home one night
drunk (often it is said)
she crowned him with a cast iron kettle
he was never quite the same
nor was her stature among his friends.

Grandmother, 1929, spun 'round town
flapper in a rumble-seat sportster, hers
dancing the Charleston
playing poker Sunday nights
Monday morning back at the office
pert secretary to the deacon of the diocese
lived four doors down
from Nellie McClung
never understood all the fuss
about that woman
in the West all women are strong
when her man died in '38
she never remarried
became her own man

a friend points her out
in the family album
the face is familiar
she plays his tables at the casino
blackjack, high and fast
sometimes two tables
talking of her grandchildren
who hearing of this
would be aghast

Mother in the 1970's
when the father leaves
it comes to this
you can't ride sidesaddle
poker face or shoot your way out
with seven children
there is no romance in this
play it straight
and they've got a jacket for you
you're tied to a table
the doctor from California
is into electricity
that lights up the last frontier
within your skull
like a Christmas tree
that will never be in season again
yours is the story
they do not tell

CONCRETE VISIONS OF CHILD

an old
old sun pokes through
fat fisted clusters of nimbostratus

through the fences picketed
around the treewalled yard
with its tin tubs floating
armadas of black-backed snappers

the red Massey rusty bedded in corn
a soup can hat on its standpipe
attended by sunflower nuns bowing head high
over hidden shrines of bricks and boards
once this was all that heaven could be

the old man across the street
all the God we'd ever need
rising sometimes from the planting of lobelia
long enough to be child again
to join the worrying of clouds
and angels with April's kites

IMAGES OF WAR

dyked by white painted shiplap
Billy's father's plot of Holland
at the end of the small street
his austere garden grew no flowers
only his family's food

this ironic immigration
from blitzkrieg memory
for on the street's opposite end
Klaus's father, former S.S. sergeant
his flower garden precise and clipped
his similar accent
drove away the neighbourhood children

while Klaus circled the street one day
in his father's black helmet
Billy retrieved revenge
from under his parents' bed
the shoebox full of old photographs
one more curled and fingerworn than the rest
a man in the leather belt of the Dutch Resistance
belted under a sash of bullets

finger set on the trigger of a machine gun
black barrel lowered on a storm trooper
kneeling hands over helmet against the wall
under the lean eye of Billy's father
who ate tulips during the war
their bulbs boiled into bitter soup

SAVAGE STONES

All the streets of our town
seemed littered
with the homemade weapons of my brothers.
Slingshots and catapults
warring on invisible enemies
from behind the buttresses of our tall green fence
that favoured daydreams of a fortress.

All the alleys then
seemed peopled by bullies or mad dogs
and my brothers ventured forth like a single weapon,
two savage stones,
tethered in a Y of cord,
half lariat, half sling,
a bolas sent hurling
with twin velocity around the neck
or leg of prey.

All their days
spent stalked or imagined stalking,
and because like deer know hunting season
or fish the shadow of a rod,
my brothers' quarry knew them.

They bagged nothing
but the nodding green Goliath
of a goose-necked streetlamp
and for years
that bolas hung there, clacking
like a stone bell

over the heads of my brothers
who had long moved on
to finer weapons.

CHRISTMAS, 1959

A storebought basket, nest of red cellophane,
a turkey and cans of plum pudding
sent home with him by the company.

And driving us to the Union's Christmas party.
His '57 Plymouth with mudflaps and rocketship fins.
The Labour Temple auditorium, folding chairs
too high to reach without his hands.
Susie in a flower pot hat
with a plastic daisy and velvet chinstrap.
And you, in a Harris tweed suit Grandmother-bought.
Little man in Buster Brown shoes and clip-on bow tie.

Not noticing him slipping away
when the light dimmed for the cartoons.
Chocolate milk in perfect miniature bottles,
sugar-dusted donuts and mandarin oranges
that peeled in sections like a map
in front of Miss Leinwebber's homeroom.

The shop steward leading choruses
of *Rudolph the Red-nosed Reindeer*.
A lady from the zoo with a real reindeer.
Three singings of *Here Comes Santa Claus*
and when he did finally, waving a white-gloved hand.

On the P.A., the names.
Finally yours, then hers.
A long way to the front without him.
When you get there, the box
full of different sized gifts in the same wrap.

A Meccano set or a tin tool box
with files, saw and a small hammer.
For Susie, who can't take her eyes
off the man in the cotton beard
with his ethered breath,
a cake mix set or nurse's kit bag
with plastic stethoscope and bottles of sugar pills.

Christmas at his house, twenty three years later,
with Sue, her children; him the grandfather.
You're an uncle. Names you never thought
you'd call each other.

No beard, but that same breath.
His eyes back there
In that scaled-down world.
Finally, you find him,
where he was all along.
Knowing he will never come home,
and why she wouldn't let go of Santa's arm.

LIGHT AGAINST LIGHT

I want again to believe
that when we love
we remain
passing always from this light
into the next.

To remember
those x-rays of my lungs
I was shown as a child
whose gauzy shadows
I thought were hidden wings.
You could feel the hot fist of the heart
but where was the soul?

And that his shoulder blades
when Billy stripped by the river
were more than bones
and that we would someday lift our arms.
We had seen the gleaned skeletons
of birds drying on the salt flats.
On each wing, a thumb and four bird fingers.

How we lost faith
and knew that the minister's collar
was a halo that had slipped,
a noose that reddened his face
and made it difficult
for him to look down.

Billy believed
that the 13 loops of the hangman's noose
made a hoop into the next life.
Me, I practiced that knot over and over.

But now there's no way back
and at night I ingest the room
and into the room, the building
and into that, the city and the lake,
until I am pulling in
all those edgeless places
where this galaxy becomes another.

Where the mind
is a sail full of light
and the body a vessel.

One day I will keep on going,
borrowed
for a lifetime,
sent spinning back.

That light I was:
all we are
luminous bodies, particles,
one against another
—light against light.

WHEN LOVE WAS A FIST

My father was handy with his hands
and a sucker for scrap.
A man who'd done hard time,
hard labour.
Determined we'd not do the same.
All seven of us.

And my grandmother who'd swoop through
on her Saturday morning visits.
A white-gloved general,
my mother hated,
inspecting the barracks.

I learned, years later,
she held the mortgage
and when my parents divorced,
sold their house
but that's another story.

One day she found
the Black Doctor
as we called it,
my father's invention,
a brute with his hands.
A man who made garages
and extra rooms for the houses we lived in.

With those same snips
he cut a man loose from a wreck,
he made a handle
and then a paddle like a cricket bat

from the thick rubber
used as baseboards in hospitals
and jails.
A tool to fix us when we broke.

I don't remember him strapping us
only my grandmother's voice
when she discovered it
and the latches used to lock us in our rooms.

I don't remember him ever using it
though he did
because I remember its sting, its weight,
and the fear
that controlled us long after that
as we waited in our rooms—
every creak of his floor
and wobble in his stairs
as he descended.

He was after all
better with snips than a hammer,
a tinsmith not a carpenter
and for that we were glad—
what he might have made of wood!

I want to tell you though
it was another time
and that my father, with this mother
and without the father you may have had
and the life he'd been given,
tried to make sense of it.

And we all called it love.

THE BEEKEEPER'S DAUGHTER

1.
Her thighs command the brute roan
cantering out of gullies
closer and faster to the fence.
Hands on the hackamore,
fist on the crop.

Mara-Daniel, blond dust
on the nape of her neck.
Her body all rumour,
jodhpurs fitted into high boots
gleaming in the stirrups
of a snotty English saddle
in cow country.

We stole down on her with binoculars,
our crotches ground into the stubble.
When she passed with a boy, we cursed;
imagined her possessed, peeled clean
damp as a willow stripling.

2.
Her father with an old country name.
Several dry acres, hives
and Mara-Daniel.

On his face, shadows of net, bees snagged.
Huge gloves reaching for the queen.
Bees clustered like dangerous grapes.

When he retired: she took up bees.
Sold the roan.
For the first time the field's plowed;
the stoneboat dragged,
boulders piled along the fence.
Boys stopped.

She became what none of us could.
More Daniel than Mara,
hair under a bandana, shoulders thickened.
Men hired for the summer.
Saturday night from passing cars
bottles hurled at the gate. Witch.

3.
Now dressed in coveralls,
she moves across the yard,
a canister of smoke lulls the bees
gorged in their hives.
Pails of honey stacked like provisions for romance.

And on Sundays, the old boys
come with their wives.
Her arms easy with the pails
along across the gate,
taking money from their wives
while the men remain in their cars
their eyes fixed on the fields.

BUT THE WIND

here in winter
that witches' wind
bares the brown shoulders of the hills
turns trees to spring
streets to rivers

skipping out at noon
in the last year of school
a silly simple plan
to slap through puddles
knee-high up down every street
was wind that opened our coats
and so took us

blame it on this odd day
April in January
your parents' empty house
an appropriate choice of music
you and your tangled hair
But the wind shook loose our clothes
sent us spinning like twin spells
tremulous through the house

PALAMINO PRAIRIE, RATTLESNAKE SUMMER

With cousin Gary
skirting gravel shoulders of Crow's Nest Pass
under the fallen face of Turtle Mountain.

Boulders on the roadside
venerable as dinosaurs
looming over the CPR tracks and across the valley
that held a town until one morning in 1903.
Whether a miner's drill,
dynamite blast or last shout of bravado,
none of that matters.
A rotten slant of rock
waiting since Noah
slid over a town in its sleep.

Eyeing the mountain I step behind him
into the stone rubble:
a cellar, wooden chairs and a candle
inside the skull of a town
mystery dank on the walls.

Fingers pinching wax from the flame
he tells me of uncle's palomino
pale sweetgrass with a sundog mane,
the hyperbole of memory.
Trucked north from the ranch at Pincher Creek
to run in the Calgary Stampede.
Driven into the rail before American tourists.
The rifle to its prize temple
where nothing is kept for beauty alone,
the utility of a bullet.

Later the uncured hide on the fence
flapping like frozen wash.
The chucked head in the gully, maggots frothy at the nostrils.
Everything in this country wind-toppled,
backed against the life.
The cable holding the barn against it,
the house leaning and uncle himself.

Homeward shushed along the highway
the colliery towns:
Frank, Bellevue, Blairmore.
Memorable bones, twisted carcasses of deer.
Stains on the road,
from the boulders they come to sun on the asphalt
being cold-blooded. Rattlesnakes, he shudders.

A road under, and around,
not a name but a nuance.
History, a mountain shouldering off centuries.
Two boys,
stone passed hand to hand.
A blade wedged in a post.
That skin spread before us
bloodied and sundried as a map
a cloud of rockdust, a shout.

JANUARY 1966 - SNOWSHOEING INTO PARADISE VALLEY

At fifteen, three miles up,
the slap of varnished rawhide.
Eyelashes frozen,
tears stinging on the cheek.

A line of boys tracking
up the sunslope's icy trail
over the wooded ridge into powder,
kneedeep in the final glissade, an alpine valley
of hoary silence, strangely small firs
and overburdened peaks.

Base camp that night,
wool steam, pine crackle,
hands drumming on tin cups.
The fooling comfort of fire
floating on a raft of logs.

A city boy takes off his snowshoes,
unnoticed, wanders off to look at stars
or some said, to piss his name in the snow.

Later the midnight search,
an erratic splinter of flashlight.
First a footstep,
one deeper, and another.
Then a tumble of snowangels
over the bank into the ravine.

And him, a body's length
from the surface.
His arms splayed as if swimming for the top,
but wrong ways up.
In his eyes the dull scud of stars,
his nostrils and mouth clotted with snow.

With his snowshoes
we dig him out.
Someone places an axe carelessly,
turns and it is gone into the snow.

Hours later, sun fills the valley.
On the toboggan, his body wrapped in a tent,
feet askew and tied with rope.

From then on, nothing what it seems,
like the trees
buried under thirty feet of snow.

JUNE 23, 1973

You found her,
you and your buddy Tom,
abandoned in an alley.
The torn ragtop, back window gone,
four flat tires, but potential there.

A few weeks shy of seventeen, swigging beer
bought by someone you asked
outside the vendor's on 37th Street.
Light in a bottle, power and speed.
Nothing can stop you.

The guy lets you have her
for a hundred bucks.
TR 6, fast as a rumour.
Tires hawked from the Goodyear.
You bring her in.
Norris, the shop teacher, looking on;
other guys in Automotives jealous,
rich kid's car.
All of you,
calling only one thing in your lives, her.

The prom three weeks away.
You were the guys without dates.
Fingernails greasy with lube;
tiny road maps of grime on your fingers.
And shop talk a front against loneliness.
Valve jobs, headers, cams.
Not engines you were talking,
but love.

Too shy to ask Charlene, at the Dairy Queen,
for anything more.

You pulled the engine, rebored her.
New rings, gaskets.
Rolling into the sunshine.
Then down to the wash on 33rd,
plates borrowed from Norris' Malibu.
A few times by the drive of the D.Q.
Charlene looking *your* way now.

When you pull the front end,
a pin sheared;
front wheel barely on.
Dealer out of stock.
Wrecker's not much better
in a town where everyone drives Fords.

What to do? You and Tom, your beer cooling;
while you huck stones at River Park.
Thursday. The prom tomorrow night.
Wire, he says. Yeah, wire.
Don't tell Norris.
Friday afternoon the pin replaced with wire.
Twisting it with pliers.
There, it won't drop.

You can hardly believe it.
New plates your brother bought.
You and Tom take her up the hill climb road
to Broadcast Hill. To the parking spot
under the radio tower over the city,
but the lot is empty before sundown.

So you cruise the bypass road.
She needs no coaxing to hit sixty.
Letting her down easy,
to the river again.
Your turf after dark.

Sometimes the rich kids, frat rats and their girls
in pleated skirts, come in convoys.
Goofs, greasers, they taunt you.
Then it's chains slapped on car hoods.
Sometimes a knuckle to nose, bone crushing
on the steps of the school. As far as it gets,
All that rage. Tonight you forget about that.

Elsewhere, others are getting ready too.
Corsages sweating in the fridge.
Dresses on the bedspread, new shoes.
You and Tom and her.
The beer is better this time.
You're confident. This power.
Won't let him take the wheel.
Later, you say, when I'm pissed.

As the sun goes down, you build a fire.
And the other loners arrive, drinking beer,
traces of their cigarettes in the dark.
Someone asks you how fast she goes.
You hadn't thought of that.
Like a challenge.

By eleven, you're on the road,
Zeppelin on the tape,
bottled light in your eyes.
Few cars this time of night.
Cops all down in the city.

The tach pops with each shift.
80-95-100
She hums.
You're soaring with her,
a road race machine that corners at 90,
into the curves.
Cutting shorter and faster
but you forget something.
The pin.

No one will say anything
until after the prom.
Charlene's there, not even noticing
you're not.
Later a few people say they wondered.

And what you couldn't have known.
How she flipped three times, the cops said.
When she lost the wheel.
Sheared a power pole.
The first news gentle.
Days pass, then the gross details.
First, through the windshield to your shoulders,
held by the dash, then snapped back again.
Your stubborn head.

And Tom they found in the bushes.
The wheel meshed in a tree.
Kids came in processions,
even the rich kids. Mortality
somehow linking you.
Too late. Vague skidmarks.
The pole already replaced. A few oil spots
fragrant with sage dust. No bloodstains.

Wanting something
to be there. To mark it.

TOWARDS A DEFINITION OF PORNOGRAPHY

One. Young men and women with degrees in English literature, living in fashionably seedy districts, writing poetry in sexually inclusive language about rape, murder, and wife-beating, all of which happens to other people.

Two. In urban clubrooms, churches, and universities, anyone engaged in politically correct discourse on pornography, violence, or Nicaragua. This is the True Story, the poem that *can* be written.

Three. My mother with a knife. This is where the definition gets personal. I am seventeen years old. She steps between my sister and my alcoholic father. That night I leave home. One year later she does. Something Margaret Atwood knows nothing about.

Four. In divorce court, the judge, two lawyers, all of them male. My mother gets one dollar a year and social assistance. My father buys a new house.

Five. My teenaged brothers in jail. For minor offences, none of them malicious. On the other side of the thick plexiglas window, their faces bruised. The elevator in the police station stopped between floors. A telephone book applied to the abdomen, the ribs. Tonight is Friday. Monday morning there will be no visible damage before the judge.

Six. The police visit my mother looking for my brothers. It is 4 a.m. This happens often. My sisters are stopped for identification checks. This too happens often. This is what they do to the lower classes in your country.

Tonight somewhere in the suburbs you are talking about us. Some of you are writing poems, taking donations, or making a film. You feel okay about this.

And my mother now goes to your churches. She has forgiven you. I have not.

IDIOT LEAVES

the sound of no sound
is not still
stone deaf
silence is weighed
in stone

when wind is a silent dance
in the court of leaves
but a flurry of august green
in the eyes of a lover
whose lips speak
no word above murmur
anonymous murmur
the crowds in the street
fall into puddles
among the mottled boulders
water trickles through wind
whose single smell
is the smell of darkness

the word
is a thought begun
found to be lost
amid embarrassed eyes
brows bent in question marks
tongues numb
with the awkward

seeing his hearing
ears filled
with the hum of small mothers
half-chant voices
and the inaudible romance
of trees brushing idiot leaves

hearing seeing
muted sounds
these twisted forms
trees finger grey clouds
sound itself
in a slow moving ballet
a precarious grace
half hints of tomorrow's storm

learning to listen
with the body
knees arthritic
nose whiskers crisp
to the days ahead
numbered deaf
and the counting
of days that matter
still hidden in the leaves
of calendars
and the unlined book

years too far
to be heard
wait like idle ears
the leaf turning
caught between the panes
of glass waiting for that chance

calm between winter's last snow
melted and spring's first rain
unfallen, a thin moon
held in the knuckled hands
of trees whose single curled leaf
is but a word
half-heard

you who ask
imagine it as you will

RAGE

"…the way people use language makes me furious. The ones who reject the colloquial & common culture. The ones who on the one hand laud the common & and denigrate the intellect, as if we are not thinking…. It takes us nowhere…"
           from *Furious*, Erin Mouré

"I'm afraid of **my** male rage,
this growing thing, this buddy, this
shadow, this new self, this stranger…"
           from *Flying Deeper Into the Century*,
           Pier Giorgio di Cicco

Hollow men indeed
our gullets empty as gulleys—
without wombs
we fill ourselves with rage
—swelling proudly.

Piling into our cars one night
because Marnie's boyfriend struck her—
racing across town
in our rage, this madness
until one by one, we slowed down
and somebody pulled over.

What each of us wouldn't admit:
pounding some sense into him
wouldn't have helped at all.

And the paunch is a lonely scream—
no place for it but our bodies
and we want to take it out, away
but we stagger on,
our belts sagging under its weight
—our potbellies glowing hubcaps
on the wheels of the body.

What we are left with—
without weapons, we beat ourselves bigger
and bigger, if there's no one else in the way—
what it means, I don't have
the damndest, but by the time it matters
in the fourteen floors of the seniors' building
there are only three of us left.

PONY CHASE

bar room cowboys in a '65 Valiant
riding out in the near west
over our shoulders a black horizon
comes in faster
than the ponies in the corral
the first gully buries the car
to its axles in mud

on foot we chase
rattling a bucket of oats
but at the first jingle of the bridle
they're off
with the storm-spooked mare in lead

finally she turns back
alongside the barn
we cut three for one last ride
ragtag on the tail end of fall

the city at our backs
over the wind-flattened fields
jotted by survey stakes
we head for the hills
and out of time
with our dude fancies
of handle-bar moustaches
tall Stetsons, woolly sheepskin chaps
he becomes Bull
i'm Shorty, the other's Red

but the ride is short
before spring thaw
the ponies will be trucked west
closer to the mountains
heavy Euclids will take to these hills
arrange them into playgrounds and streets
where children playing cowboys
hear the rumble of ghostherds

back in town at the bar
we come down bowlegged and dreambent
knowing, 250 Detroit horses
will never match
one mangy pony

AND I LAY DOWN IN A FIELD OF WHEAT

The summer I was homeless.
Between school
and whatever comes next,
on the brink of forever.

The road stark with possibility
all the way to the vanishing point.
Riding into Saskatchewan
green wheat waist high
dropped off at night between towns
walking an hour hungry towards that lone light
until I lay down,
young wheat around me, carefully parted it.
Sheltered as the wind brushed its bristles
spinning in my sleep freed of gravity
one by one tapping the stars.
My face rain-spotted and delirious.

At daybreak the first car stops.
Ten miles to a gas station and that damn light
that beckoned large and clear as a false moon.

Where is he now, that boy,
under the ears of wheat
that catch his whispers,
hitching north to Canora.
17 Kamalkoffs in the book
the second one he calls,
Ruby's my cousin.
Farm's just out side of town.

A furred brown bee chases him and he ducks
as she walks towards him laughing.
Come visit me, she'd said at graduation.
Her father sends him packing after lunch,
a paper bag of sandwiches and a bottle of milk
and he's glad for it
as he puts out his thumb
heading for the Minnedosa Valley
because it's green, it's a name he'd never heard
and a place he'd never been.

SKYHOOKS

And now, mid-week, mid-life,
with my brothers and their children
in the foothills above the city of our birth.
With our bright skyhooks—a name
better saved for these kites:
a skyful of flying ruckus
in the reckless wind
off the Rockies—a red box,
a flying blue carp and fighting dragon tails.

Each of them angling for light,
strung between existence and dream
trolling for skyfish or errant angels
lost in the lure of the clouds.

Thirty years past,
my first job and that apprenticeship
—how I went to the foreman
when they sent me off to find
that mythical tool—the skyhook,
every apprentice sent chasing,
like left-handed monkey wrenches, queafy tape
or scurpan dimmers
—while the journeymen guffawed.
But my father's stories warned me.

Told the foreman I wasn't going back
until I had one
and we made up a box
and a bill of lading, labelled it boldly.

The journeymen stood big-eyed
as boys, wanting to believe.
No one had ever come back with one.
Maybe there *was* a skyhook afterall.

Until the box torn open
revealed a rod I'd bent into a question mark
with a loop on the end
and disappointed, they chased me
for playing the joke backwards.
And here, now on a windy hill,
so much behind us, my brothers softer now
than our father, the future has come for us.

Deep sky above, the laving of prairie below.
In our hands the sorcery of strings
summoning fishes and loaves, whatever we want,
the old stories we've almost lost:
all the possibilities of belief
and sky.

THE TIMEKEEPING GHOSTS

April it begins, the mongrel pain
longing already for this place
i am about to leave
hometown this ancestral stopover
where my great grandfather filed claim
on the homestead for the brothers
father who waited in the east

four sections at the junction
of the Bow and Highwood rivers
they never came
unable to return, he began the house
the family, two daughters and a son
one of whom was to marry
ride from the ranch with a husband
who would die in less than six years
leaving her with a son
and a lifetime to spend mourning
a lover, a marriage that was never
but more perfect
with each passing season

my father that son
would leave too in time
the newer house in town
with a barn that housed the Model T
the one in the family album
(he still has the toolbox
that sat on the running board)
by now he is easy with his mementoes
in this place of windy hills

not far from the junction
the stopover becoming more permanent
where the plank washed loose in flood
wedged between two aspens
(the farm chosen for pastoral splendour
was a flood plain)
they talk about that in my family
my grandmother, my father
pictures in the family album

we are a people of small things, our histories
saved in pictures, boards and toolboxes
i have a meat grinder long past use
my grandmother, a brick
with a picture of the house from which it came
taped to the top

he must have known that like him we
were bound to these ludicrous places
by slivers, boards, all that is left
this grinder, my grandmother's metaphors
these bricks and pictures

i will break this curse of years
do as you wish
go back go forward
(i am your mirror, your image reversed)
i have the watch engraved
with your name/mine
i will go east past the junction
the dust of the house
the timekeeping ghosts
past the pictures
past this place

THE THORN GARDEN

CHARLIE'S POEM

his story of the lady
forty years with the company
when she retired last year

forgetting even the watch
instead they planted
a dollar and a half tree
in her honour
but the dogs
sensing the brevity of these things
raised only legs in salute
and a tree falls
far short of a lifetime

TALL TALK

first day on the job that last long winter
in the lunchroom waiting for the 8 o'clock horn
talk is tough and hairy
there's a sign:
IT'S HARD TO SOAR LIKE AN EAGLE
WHEN YOU WORK WITH TURKEYS
the biggest of the crew
a foot and a fur hat over me
pokes a long finger into my chest
after my job?
he thumbs towards the rest
they all are

i'm no hero and when the foreman appears
wiser in the ways of these things
sends me out as this guy's driver
it begins with turns
on truck and loader, the tensile trust
with two tons of steel overhead
we have little choice thawing
over coffee, frozen fuel lines
after meetings at the union hall
recounting meaner winters, stories, old lines
all the while crafting new ones into our faces
with arms locked in mock wrestle

ICON IN RYE

his retirement party
they're staging it like a crucifixion
at sixty-three retirement forced
with wine and cheese for the guy
who always drank rye out back
with the boys from shipping
the boss is there standing guard
over the old man full of bile and cancer
who calls me aside:
son of a bitch
that's not wine
but blood he's drinking
my blood

the ladies from the kitchen
there among his friends
few despite the show of president
vice presidents and various secretaries
finally it's time
they roll in the cake
on the cart full of gifts
among them the obligatory watch

later he tells the guys from shipping
a watch?
me, i got no use for time
they nod and under the table
top the wine glasses with rye

DIESEL HAIKU (OCCIDENTAL)

5 a.m.
painted windows
dark in drift
the phone rings
it's the Wind calling
snow call
for the plough driver

long white day waiting
for the curve
of the ploughman's blade

SNOWPLOW DRIVER'S DREAM

it's the crew boss: *big storm last night
so we're calling the crews in early*
and me in from my dream
of a skeletal ship in distant clouds
where she holds aloft a single card
she is not my other or a lover
the card is the queen of spades

past the curtains in frosted windows
day is a ghost-ridden horizon
trees sway in windy choreography
i hear a laughing roar
as she cocks her dark head
lifts haughty skirts in storm
today i will watch my roads
for the scuffed tracks of a black dancer—
that card she holds is mine

BILLY NO LONGER THE KID

mean and mouthy
tough man on the cemetery crew
going for low
but the dead and those nearly
the old guys don't care

at twenty
proud of the fact
he's hot shit on the backhoe
(you can tell by the way he wears his hat
CAT diesel, high off his forehead)

neck red with more than sun
under the striped tank top
gut already roly
from too many lunchroom beers
at the U.A.W. hall

the other day
one tree in the entire place
he hits it in third gear
it takes two trucks
to pull the bucket from the trunk

Billy hatless
broken glasses and nose bloodied
old Carlos tells him
what he already knows
what's the hurry
you're gonna get here soon enough

SONG FOR THE QUARRYMEN

All day in gumboots I stand
among the flowers with a hose
while it rains not nearly enough for any good.

To those first settlers
a practical place for a graveyard,
next to a quarry. A short haul from town
for stone and dead.

They are all here now
and I somewhat solemn in their presence
and the rain and their work.
Of that, the young magnolias or recent yews,
only tall oaks and red maples
over the road to the Welland Canal.

And the trees
nowhere in this garden city so green.
Reverend Sir or local madman
no better the bones of one than another
for the roots that mingle through the graves.

Dusty miller, choleus, allysum,
I water, coerce with sphagnum and fungicide.
Decay already everywhere here. At night
I peel layers of dead skin
from my feet, a wart has taken root.

Feeling like the quarrymen,
their first marker dated 1847,
cutting stone finally for their own graves.

At times it seems
each wet leaf offers not a reflection
but a face sent up from the roots.
Stone remembers the living, not the dead.
I read instead the leaves,
my fingers moving along their stippled ribs.

Around me the stonecutter's work:
the shrouded urns, a marble heart
hanging like a locket.
Fieldstone, granite, local and Italian marble,
plaster, cement. The epitaphs:
*Forever at Rest, Here Lies, Rest
in Peace. Forever Asleep with Jesus,
Dearly Missed, Beloved Wife of.*

Last of the stone cut in the '30's
for arches and stone stairs
running down to the lagoon in the old quarry,
with its seven weeping willows,
now backfilled with a dry bed of impatiens.

From raceme vines over the arches
I gather wet bunches of roses
for the woman in the office.

At four the carillon's recorded bells
from the stone tower—*Rock of Ages*
the last three bars offkey.
I roll up my hoses.
A freighter sounds entering the lock.

Rain-dappled my skin always,
nostrils open and close
around the leaf-rot warmth of the greenhouse.
The odour of rain, worms and summer.

DEEP IN THE SOUTH OF MY COUNTRY

As gangs such bastards,
alone we are little more.
Only our fears civilize us.

This hard town of steel plants,
car factories and white vats of chemicals.

But a sign on the freeway says:
The Garden City.

The head gardener drives me around
the first week before I am given the key
to the cemetery's iron gates.

Stopping off to introduce me
to the crews huddled over coffee in donut shops.
Men with names like Antonio, Jimmy, Raoul,
hats easy on the backs of their heads.
Low talking,
louder when they hear I'm okay
meaning I come down
on the side of the union.

Last winter's long strike,
negotiations falter
in a town where thousands are out.

On the coldest night, some of them
air-conditioned the house of a scab,
with bricks through every window.

Or how a foreman, followed home one night,
stepped from his truck.
A shotgun blast, no one knows who,
took out the back window,
a warning.

These men, their wives
swollen with a first child or second,
banded in fear.

SPRING OPENING—LOCK FOUR

After hours
on the grass banks of the Welland.

Drinking Billy's whisky,
squinting at black-bottomed lakers
downbound out of Erie.
Glare of white funnels,
idle deck gantrys and radar's easy lope.

Six of them squat in the current
where the lazy willows fan.
Their sailors smoking at the rails
watching leggy women with cameras
on the lock walls.

When the siren goes, six horns sound
and a ship descends
like a toy boat in a drained bathtub.

Water spills from the sluice,
spring shipping opens
with the great iron gates.

The stack shudders,
pops a cloud of diesel
as the iron-loaded laker
pulls for Montreal.

Beside me, Billy tilts the empty bottle
stares through the long neck
as if we're all sailors

set on this plank of earth,
this side of the telescope,
drifting towards that one day
when we wish we were elsewhere.

One of the sailors sees us
and waves. Billy blows across the bottle's neck,
like a ship's horn,
his eye ringed with whisky and spit.

THE MOWER MAN

Sun over the low stone wall
framed in the pillars of the freeway
rising over the canal.

The gravediggers tell me
of a she-rabbit's flattened body
in the road that cuts the veterans' section.
The other dead are theirs,
mine somehow is the realm of animals and trees.

In the field beside the workhouse
old Bill, with one short leg and a brace,
grabs the young guy's balls
until the foreman whistles.

Then with the racket of his five gang mower,
one long eyebrow over inset sockets
peering into the stone tunnels ahead,
he becomes the mower man.

Roaring into spring, sixty twisted blades
shearing over the green billowing stuff between the rows.
His squat arms are ricochets of flesh
as the mower bounces over the mounds.
Floating reels churning in the green foam.
All spring into fall he will rally over the graves.

From the cenotaph's tattered flags,
a day that begins innocent as war,
fake poppies on tipped-over wire stands.
I am walking with the body of the she-rabbit in a box
when he passes and it happens.

Blood spins onto his white t-shirt.
Reels red, fur bits fly from the blades.
The next of the mother sheared in half.
One of them flipped and slit
two remaining dart to the next stone.

Wiping blood from his face
he helps me catch them in his coat.
The others, what is left, and the mother
we bury in a hedgerow
on the edge of the veterans' section.

Above the fur-lined collar of the next,
the stone marked DIEPPE 1944.
How it is always, the same sun,
the carelessness of men.

The shadow of the mower man
limping towards the shop.
Under his jacket, their lungs
flapping against their ribs.

THE THORN GARDEN

Down the stone stairs
blocked into the hill
to the roses in the pit of the old quarry
by the lagoon
with its seven weeping willows.

All is past
in the oldest quarter of the cemetery.
Wind-sheltered roses speckled with rot.
Spider webs spangled with flies.

Below the grassy berm
shelves of quarried-out stone,
hillocks of dry brome, lockspar,
and nettle that shreds my sleeves.

My knuckles crack
as roots older than a season
jar the hoe which sparks on stone.
Despite orders I'll leave them
as did every gardener before me.
Not hating but admiring these cocky weeds;
easy enough to love a rose.

A tumbledown joy
in all this maudlin order,
stubborn fans of portulaca,
stands of pearly everlasting,
and dogstrangling vine.
Fleabane, coltsfoot
speeding towards the neat mown graves.

This garden of sickly roses.
The haze of June,
a wet handkerchief over my mouth.
Yellowjackets hanging like angry yellow heat
over the green rubble of the south-facing slope.

THE WORM

Carlo the Calabrian gravedigger
calls them beetles
as they crawl through the gate, headlights on,
roar out the back leaving wooden loads.

He calls his friend, the undertaker, Worm.
For no other reason
than when you've stared
into the open ground this long
things appear that way.

The Worm told him how it's done,
Carlo remembers in disgust,
his details are too precise.

How the hair grows from the ears,
from the nose, over the lips.
Nails surge,
the penis lifts
one last triumphant farewell
and the Worm snaps it with a heavy brush
used to settle the hairs of the dead.

Jaws wired through the teeth,
lips sealed with glue or stitched.
On the eyeball, a spiked cup
hooks the eyelid over the cold gaze.

Sunken faces padded with cotton.
The crushed skull filled with pounds of wax,
blue pallor of death powdered over.
The Worm arranges their smiles.

But I tell my wife, Carlo says,
to leave it standing tall
with a wreath around it.
At the mass put her lips,
like a good Catholic
to my Roman candle.

BETWEEN THE OLD AND THE KNOWING

Slightly elegant
in a tilted rambunctious way
with a noble sweep
one pace across and another tall.

Not overlooked by the young gardener
who knew no better
watered well, weeded around.

No doubt marvelled over,
the flower vaguely Oriental,
ruffled pods, rucked leaves,
a sure stem.

Until the old gardener
with all the grip
the old have on the young,
seizes it, lifts,
exposing the shallow and ridiculous root.
Age has made him sure of this one thing.

Heaped onto the trash pile
loudly and without a word
proclaimed: weed.

FOUND ON A SUNDIAL DATED APRIL 14, 1936

Alas, you say,
time goes.

Ah no!

Time stays,
you go.

WHAT THE DEAD DREAM

The newspaper stories of the end:
white lights, threshold's crossed,
pearly gates, Maker's met.
Told always of course
by those who've come back.

But if I were a medieval gardener
I'd tell you how it starts
from the brow,
the hair that snakes upward.
And that the dead's dreams are green,
rooted in the skull.
Rows of them and on certain nights,
say nearer the full moon,
the ground thrums with their thoughts.
Their bones click shuffle
on the spot.

What do the dead dream?
I don't know.
Perhaps their dreams are open
taking in all of us.
But I know what I see.
The leaves of those dreams
talking in colours and perfumes.

Maybe they dream forward
not back ward.
The problem with memory—
stuck with what's happened
when the dead as the living do
need what's next.
It must be
they're dreaming to meet us.

I know, because over and over
the trees repeat their warning.
Green shout of spring,
winter's one hand bargaining.
Each spring I trowel in the gaudy annuals
a little less hearty,
and Thanksgiving, I count my friends.

HAWK ON A SHROUDED URN

From the woodlot she flies in,
morning and dusk,
over the graves.
Her winged shadow beside me.

Her slow circular lope
until she's squat on the air.
Wings tucked
along the pink-banded belly.

That cry:
kerr kerr,
and the sudden plummet.
Whether talons
or the stunned blow of her
that kills.

Talons I've seen only
when the zoo's falconmaster
tosses meat, hooked and slashed
before it lands.

She alights sometimes
on a stone shrouded urn
on the tallest column.
Her head pivoted, left then right.
One eyelid flapping
over stone globes of sky and green.

When a blade or twig moves,
she drops.
Wings splayed
an umbrella stopped
short of the ground.

And then sprung
steep over the trees
to a nest of sticks,
a shadow dangling in her grip
for the young
in that dead oak across the canal.

THE ROSES

My lunch shaded in the wheelbarrow
under trees whose leaves
have flipped upside with heat.
Flies hang stuck on the air.
Factories to the north silent on the noon whistle.

At my back, cold stone stairs.
To each side, roses, their red lobes
and shimmery hips jostle my face
with a sultry attar that dares me.

My knife hooks under the skin
of the damp speckled orange.
Its juice sears my lips,
spills to the hair of my belly.

From my near-stripped body
wafts sweat, oranges and crushed grass
mingling with the musk of my semen,
the brine scent of a woman last night.

Morning recalled with its open windows.
A breeze over our backs, sharp as the roses.
Love's only delicacy, sleeping,
then the slow lift, the arch, the pounding.

How many lovers lie below,
forgotten smells, feather pillows,
canopied beds or straw ticks of the lovemaking.
What do the stones say of this
and lovers who watched the ships of summer
on the Welland Canal.

I break the orange into easy crescents,
juice sticking my fingers,
stuff my mouth with them,
test their fruit between my teeth.
The slow rise begins again,
roses around me
faint red murmurs in the standstill air.

Hard as a plum
my cock appears under my cutoffs,
straining towards the roses,
mindless of the thorns.

And I bend the rose,
arc into its velvet cusp.
In my back begins the familiar tightness,
the almost pain of the strings drawn on every muscle.
Sweat trickles down my nose,
the cool rose in my coarse brown hands.

Against the stone the pummel of bone.
Our skins do not release us
like the plum holds its pulp
within a tautened skin.

My semen in the throat of the rose,
for a moment, I forget,
our urging, hard driving at the petalled doors
of our skins, stone piled
on the chests of the dead.

The orange peel lies
against the dying grass of summer
like a continent against a map's sea.
Petals slipping wet
between my fingers.

THE SCALE

Dawn's lightning in the treetops
charged with nitrogen.
Air punky with electricity.
The crown of an old chestnut split.

Lifted into the damage,
angel of mercy in a hardhat.
Distant thunder, wind enough
to make this a warning of worse.
A thunderbolt gashed the trunk
and what isn't burned is broken.

Cable locked in.
The chainsaw bucks back,
each limb clatters down the trunk.
Chain oil slick on my face,
fingers quiver on the trigger.

My chest buckles in the sharp air.
Lodged in its own quarters,
a bad surprise that could explode someday
in the hands of a surgeon,
if I'm lucky there'll be enough to mend.

The winch driver below
old hand with chains and diesel engines.
Both of us aware the cable's
strung tight as a guitar string,
what the tree's weight is
to the fibreglass bucket or the truck's cab.

Stepping on a branch
the girth of the safety belt
keeps me belly to bark.
Each change of wind
pitches the cable to a high hum.
The driver stands by.

Always we rough house,
downplaying the soft touch on the lever
where megatons of hydraulic can kill.
Here the scale of gentleness is giant.

Down to the live sections
the trunk is winched shut.
The auger churns into heartwood,
sand to cinnamon colour.

The drill forced my chest
into a pulse not mechanical
that syncs with my own from shoulder to glove
a steel thread I'm strung on.

Ruminations of the dead
for whose hands these trees are gloves
pressing the sky I'm perched in
closer to their grey dumb skulls.

When the drill breaks through,
my chest thuds.
Four holes every two feet,
threaded rod malleted,
capped with washers, huge bolts.

Shreds of bark tugged clean,
deeper fissures chiselled smooth,
sure-handed as any bedside Michelangelo.
Dressed with tar, a hundred years of tree.

The tree sways
top heavy with my weight
and the tension of metal.
My back on a limb,
feet dangle in arboreous clouds.

On the ground, tools in alcohol.
What virus this one had,
they'll carry to the next.
This contraption of leaves
hanging on chance and hammered sutures.

The tremor is quiet.
When it comes,
so much depends on the muscle
the eye and the cut.

THE GROUNDHOG'S CURSE

He ambles into the air
from his clay door to the sunken mounds.
Grizzled and addled
on his fat haunches.
Snorting at all this light.

Below him, collapsed catacombs
of pine and oak.
Whole rooms waddled through,
fanned roots and shredded cloth.
His coat slick
with the stink of there.

The young gravediggers despise his irreverence,
what he must know.
Moving like a spirit
in a slow motion that dares.

One day they circle him.
Only then he wheezes
in something like fear.
His old eyes blink stupidly at theirs
as they flatten him again and again
with their shovels.

His body heaped on the truck.
One gloved paw,
upturned and open.
His lair backfilled.
The men giddy with killing.

THE FUNERAL

The thunderstorms of August,
I am no longer safe.
The ground cleaves,
each stone is an unplugged mouth,
each row a choir confessing.
I am afraid, descending darkly
the stone stairs into the garden's thorns.

Out of rain's heavy stage curtains
the sound of hoofbeats
on the cobblestone road from town.
Somewhere a truck backfires.

Hoofbeats?
And the remnants of the road
visible only where worn tar
reveals paved-over stone.

Out of the parted folds of rain
comes the black horse, the landaus
and the horse-drawn hearse.
A widow bustled in black.
The gilt and ribboned badges of mourners
and the undertaker in stovepipe hat.
The glistening livery of a dozen carriages.

Under the canopy,
in quick succession: the eulogy,
the parson empties a pouch of earth,
the daughter places a rose,
the box nailed shut.

Later the stone on a wagon
upended and roped into place.
The name not near enough to read.
Then thunder again
and through the rain, the sun.

A truck door slams in the 20th century.
Two men in yellow slickers
appear like flames following the dark.
And this past, ever-parting
hoofbeats on the road to town.

THE YOUNG WIDOW

To her, invisible as a church janitor;
even the jangle of my tools, nothing.

She allows me a shadow's closeness.
Her hair so tight
as if one face is pulled over another.
In the car, three children
too young for reverence.

Behind the alyssum
tamped out of plastic cubes,
she leaves an envelope.

When they leave,
I read the letters
a child's hand makes.
A homemade card with a house,
one fuzzy tree, three stick children,
two parents in front
with clouds coming out of the chimney.
Sunday, I remember, is Father's Day.

In the order of miracles,
there is nothing I can do.
But the simple flowers live
through the July drought,
watered against regulations
when the super isn't looking.
The envelope settles into the soil.

And if anything happens at all,
she visits in a year
or two, in another car
or the same one, with the children or not,
perhaps alone
or with a man who looks uncomfortable.

She may plant a small tree
but there will be no flowers.
This is the last time.
Her shoes tapping away on the road.

BASEBALL OF THE BIZARRE

Between full moons
and the busy seasons of Christmas and Easter
when the dying take their time,
the gravediggers amuse themselves
with card tricks or twig puzzles
under the buckeye tree.

But strange Raoul, the mute Portuguese trucker,
in his numbered shirt and black ballcap,
who crosses himself before each digging,
flips his pearl-handled stiletto
at a circled board.
The blade honed on a tombstone,
tested on his tongue.

Tired of that,
he practises for the city's team
copping flies from the blue lunchroom air.
Hurled to the floor from his fist,
they bounce brightly
two feet into the air and dead.
The floor underfoot crummy with flies.

Outdoors, with the drama of a B-league pitcher,
dozey yellowjackets from his skin
chucked at the foreman
like a baseball of the bizarre.
When they talk of his throw, the misfit curve,
Carlo the sly one calls it
the red centipede stitched on the white skin
that splits at the bat.

And how with the dark buzz of revenge,
one wing, segmented eyes, a thorax,
then thousands and thousands of them
funnel into the sky
—the flyball of strange Raoul.

TEN THOUSAND JAWS

Under the pear tree,
sun-festered circles of windfall.
And the wasps flicker
over the ripe mash of summer.

On the radio:
a boy in Michigan
walking his dog
stumbles on a nest.
The leash looped round a tree,
they fall, covered.
Both of them die.

What is not said:
that wasps have not only stingers,
but mandibles or jaws,
can bite again and again;
how they are attracted
to water, raw meat, fruit;
have the ability to reason.
There are ten thousand in a nest.

And around my face they flare
close as lit cigarettes.
I move deliberately
so they consider me not the fruit
but the tree.

MAGNOLIA FRASERI WALT

Belle of the trees.
That perfumed bark,
ear-shaped leaves list in the breeze.
But the dusky and celebrated blossom
wilts in the first searing days of summer.

Not the flower but the seed endures,
October's hard fruit,
hairy green and wrinkled beak,
eyeless head of a green bird
begins its loaded arc.

Whose damp brain pops
a loud seed like a bright red thought
to wobble in the pod.

Until the wind shakes
and it drops before the leaves do.
They and snow press it into the ground.

In spring, one green plume
and another tendril,
slip through the cracked earth.

The slow soar of another tree.
In seven years
a pale bloom trills.

THEY DREAM OF BEING GARDENERS

Among smoking piles of leaves
the gardeners stash straw and pig manure
around the roses to overwinter.
On the curbside, gutted flowers
are forked onto the truck.

Leaves rattle down my neck,
acorns poke my knees,
as boxfuls of tulips, crocuses
are placed into the forked-over soil
with the heels of the hands.

Bone meal dust lifts into the eyes, the nose.
Everywhere burned and broken bone
poured around each bulb.

The gravediggers talk of the stench
of death, when a body is exhumed.
The backhoe cutting through the watertable
unleashes the wash of graves uphill
and an unholy mist rises from the pit.
A smell that remains for days
in the windless hollow of the cemetery,
on the clothing, in the nostrils.

With each bulb, the burial of some animal part.
The nostrils turn with the stomach.
The smell of smoke and bone.

The other gardeners see themselves
as better than the gravediggers,
who must leave their coveralls
outside the lunchroom,
whose wives will not have them
on those days when the old graves are opened.

But none of them dares look
into the mouths of the graves
just as the gravediggers do not touch the roses.

And the gravediggers dream of being gardeners
having filled too many holes with the dead.
The reminder always too much,
their eyes like plumb bobs
on the surface of this life,
plummet with every shovelful
into the stinking water of the swimmers
in the lake under our feet.

WARLOCK'S ARSENAL

No cure for its alchemy
not even a one-legged man
running for the coast.

When the old guys hork blood
Bill the young gardener glares. Chemicals.
Told in training
the thin membranes of the eyes
direct entry into the bloodstream.
Under the mask and goggles
you breathe uneasy, your throat
heavy with phlegm.
They laugh at your precautions.

All our stories
of this foreman or another:
so safe you can drink it.
Five years later, banned.
2-4-5 T, Agent Orange by another name.

The slow casualties,
symptoms passed off as living.

Downstairs in the shop,
a cabinet that Carlo calls
the warlock's cupboard.
Broken bags of green powders,
brown bottles labelled
with skull and crossbones.
Can't dump it.
Too old to use; who knows
what it is. Can't bury it.

You try to forget what you know:
two years ago
spraying upwind of the school.
Wind rises and falls. Had your orders.
Fog drifts. Diapers flagging
on the lines in the new suburbs.

Outside the supermarket
a woman sells plastic lapel pins
and daffodils tilted in buckets.
While your nostrils rankle
somewhere between dairy products and produce
the unmistakable stink of 2-4 D,
yellow bags of Weed and Feed.

Then over the line one night
looking for a bar in Niagara Falls, New York.
The year after Love Canal;
the year before someone discovers
toxins in the Lakes.
Like a shrine
at the end of the street,
high white tanks spotlighted:
      HOOKER CHEMICALS
You turn down another,
that ends in white tanks
and another, until you're lost in them.
Nowhere to turn.
You drink more beer that night.

You wake up
sweat under your chin;
that July in a rubberized suit,
you'd pulled down your mask for awhile.
How many gallons of sour air
in your clothes, your skin.

Blood tests. Will they find it
when they don't know
what they're looking for.

Monster cells and the fear
splitting and devouring,
until your skin no longer contains you.

SELECTED CANADIAN RIFLES

Some say
this country
is ruled by wind alone.
There are only the odds
pitted
against cold
hunger/the land.
Our only contenders
in this struggle.

Remember
Nanaimo 1858
wooden wagons tumble
glass bottles of nitro-glycerine
on the trails
in the mines
miners die.
One by one.
The coal company
with government contracts to fill
preaches fire.
Negotiations begin
a flutter of militia rifles
the miners retreat
consider the choice.

Nanaimo 1913
Deaths number over a hundred.
The miners rise again.
Redcoats mark the edges
of night with bayonets.
Shots fall upon the miners.
For some memory
forever erased.

Winnipeg 1919
Bakers, sweepers, blacksmiths
join the unemployed in protest
fists are clenched like hammers.
Winnipeg shuts down in strike.
The rifles barely dusty
are raised
this time against the men
who held them in a war
a year forgotten.

Bienfait cemetery
near Estevan
truth and time marked in stone
over a common grave

      MORGAN
     MARKUNAS
     GRYSHKO
MURDERED IN ESTEVAN
 SEPTEMBER 29, 1931
    BY R.C.M.P.

The rifles miss children and women
in the angry crowd
but their fathers, husbands
fail to return.

Regina 1935
low brow winds spit dust
in the eyes of the Mounties
as they ride to music
for rifle and bayonet
against farmer and hobo.
Blood the only rain
that falls among the thistle
that year.

Pearl Harbour 1941
Even the silent
the meek are not exempt.
Before the finish
of the counting of American dead
the rifles turn inward.
The enemy is suddenly among us.
Trucks buck the south Alberta wind
with Japanese prisoners.

October 1970
Montreal, Vancouver
Moose Jaw
war measures
an even vaguer enemy.
Police and television men
on the screen.
He is white
he is among us.
Which one of us
is he?

Ipperwash 1995
The guns rattle again
on the Chippewa
on the land that was always theirs
above the sands of Lake Huron.
Orders come one night,
thirty cops and one dead Indian
as the geese migrate south
over the burial ground
he defended.
Hush, hush, can you hear them?

MEDITATION ON THE IMPROBABLE HISTORY OF A SMALL TOWN

Hate Teacher Convicted Again
July 17, 1994

Midway between Red Deer
and Rocky Mountain House on Highway 11.
Eckville pop. 800
and Jim Keegstra.
Former auto mechanic, former
school teacher, now auto mechanic again.

The original settlers recognizing potential
in the belly above the Bible belt
called it Hell
under their breath.
Grasshoppers, drought,
and mosquitoes
when it finally did rain.

But it's not the kind of name
that goes on a C.P.R. map
in a fine new country.
What about Heck, someone offered.
Too obvious said another.
Someone else: Heckville.
A remittance man
with a sense of humour,
so the township papers came back
Eckville.

What happened here
happens in every small town.
Some born, some died, most
moved away.

Until a man taught history
the way you rebuild engines:
do a bit here,
drop this, add that
and what you don't have
make yourself. Found himself teaching math:
six million equals zero.
No one saw anything,
not the principal nor the school board.

And when the trial's over
and the reporters go back
to Toronto or Calgary or Tel Aviv,
the principal and the superintendent
still there and the name
Eckville.

Although sometimes
it must be Hell.

THE DAY WE TORE UP STANLEY'S LAWN

The neighbours thought we were crazy.
And so did we.
As the naked clay dried
and the wind off Kalamalka Lake
swirled it in our faces.

And the bare lines of the irrigation pipe
lay like a grid on a brown map
of the West,
the windy West, the West of twenty year droughts,
the West that was never green,
where hard pan is dry ten feet down.

The neighbours came to watch
and a police car stopped by
—he'd had a complaint
but there's no law against tearing up your lawn.

Drinking Stanley's beer until dusk
sitting on the mounds of dying sod
we started on the dinner's wine
and stared at each other,
began pulling up the plastic grid.

Brass nozzles fell on the driveway,
black pipe curled around us
and we whooped
and Stanley the iron man yanked hard
and we both pulled.
We'd caught something,
so we tugged again

and up came a man who'd been watering his driveway
and there were three of us now
and Stanley's wife and kids,
we all pulled hard
and heard a distant rumble,
as lights went off around the lake
—we'd bagged the dam
and freed the river.

All night it went on
and that one went down to free another
and another, over the Great Divide,
the Brazeau, the Oldman, the Whitegoat.

Lights went off all over the Northwest,
as the Columbia, the Cascade,
the San Fernando, the Colorado,
down along the Great Divide,
rivers smacking down the squatter's shacks,
and their kidney-shaped pools
and all the putting greens of Arizona.

Everywhere people came out to watch
the rivers come back.

We've started something, Stanley said.

We waited,
wondering what next,
and perfected a new sport,
whirling it high and around us,
tossing the lawnmower over our heads
like a four-wheeled caber.

And all around our feet
there was new growth:
sweetgrass, brome,
fescue and wild rose.
The earth began to smell again
the day Stanley pulled the plug.

We'd broken the green spell
that Eastern green, that English curse.
And the new colours now:
yellows, the gold of palomino,
of sundogs, greys and adobes.

Hoofbeats we heard one night.
No, Stanley said,
but I heard them too
and the sky fluttered
dark with birds coming back
and the earth shook.

And all the impatient farmers went back
to the green and possible East,
and the Impossible West was quiet and golden again.
No pump jacks, no farms,
the West the way it was.

And Stanley's new lawn spread
like a tumbleweed blowing across the West
the Northwest, the Southwest,
the golden West.

And now the wind blows,
light as prairie clover,
sweet as sage.

SEASONS OF THE CITY

MY STREET

Here on this fabulous street
where I am never alone, the deaf man,
not the dumb man, wired,
my ears full of microphones:
the tick of streetcars tracking by
as a crowd gathers to enter
the fantastic purple walls of a night club.

But the show begins in the street
when Katie the barker yells:
"cock, fuckass, police"
and a man in black leather
with a steel hook for a hand
spears an apple for his girlfriend.

And between the tattoo parlour
where the bikers drill their arms
with skulls and daggers
and the window of Sister Waneita, Reader of Stars
where a tiger tabby crouches among the snake plants,
a man who resembles Karl Marx directs traffic
and curses the buses that roar back
while Jimmy and his pal Roberto
race electric wheelchairs down opposite sides of the street.

And the Portuguese huddle to mass
while a fat hooker drops into an expensive Ford
and a shirtless man driven towards somewhere
slamdances into the crowd that parts for him
as Gibson the blind guy peddles sunglasses
and whistles at all the girls
and yells: "Baby, I can *smell* you're beautiful."

And a man with no legs
knuckles his way on a wheeled board
then tucks it and ascends the stairs
with a swagger that has legs
into the Galaxy Donut Shop
to drink with the man with no arms
who upends a cup with his teeth.

And the beautiful man who plays guitar
with a withered hand,
the women buy his poetry as he blesses them.
On this street, the droolers laugh
at the scab-armed girl who burns herself
and she laughs back.
The cleft argue with the mute in furious wet sputters.
When we greet you on my street
we look for your wires
your scars.

SEASONS OF THE CITY

Between sunrise and moon-set,
beach and watermark, between
quadrants, north and south
between jazz and more jazz, smoke
and fire, hail and snow, portentous
and sublime, between rain and lightning,
subterfuge and centrifuge, between buckeyes
and sumac, between Bathurst
and Tecumseth.

All the seasons of the city,
between the sated and starved—the malnourished
die content and the conservatives
enjoy their steaks only if others are hungry.
Between the bread and the circus, between Baudelaire
and Bachelard—the spaces of the spaced
on night, on the speed of light.

Between the pious and the pitied, between
a curse and a prayer; my God,
it's not the commitment that counts
it's the tone.

Between darkness and light-blindness, between
dead and dying, grieving and aggrieved,
born and bearing, spinning with the seasons.
Like that dream of my youth
dizzy with vertigo from the spinning planet;
without pull, I'm earth-freed,
space bound, out of gravity
beyond fear.

And I awake always, I swear,
having touched the ceiling
my lungs full of light.

DECEMBER ARSON IN CABBAGETOWN
(FOR ANDREW WREGGETT)

Allure, always
both soft and metallic,
like sex
like a steel blade against the throat,
like a hammer and a nail
ticking against the fillings of our teeth.

As much as we love
one so differs from another
that there can be no universal wisdom,
no True North of the Heart,
no magnetic field that points us
heartward
homeward.

But always that one True Thing
we are, finally,
always, always alone with our lost allure
ticking like a blade
or a bomb.

And sitting in a donut shop on Parliament Street
December 24 a few years ago,
reading your letter "…She left…."
This much we know,
but instead, I want to make you laugh.

Like, love is a donut:
when she's eaten the rest
and left you the hole.
But serious business, this angst,
this love stuff that can kill us.

And besides it's thirty below,
the pathetic fallacy not mine,
but an arsonist's
who torched the house
across the street last night.

And the firemen still lumber through the ruins,
in frozen yellow jackets,
ravaged timber steaming into black crystal
and for a raw moment

I see the clarity of ruins
and like our mutual friend, Camus,
I am shivering, breathless
in the presence of such beauty.

NEAR ST. JAMESTOWN CEMETERY

All night in the arms of the city
watching the man
who spins swans and reindeer
out of torched glass,
snipping and tying
as the street goes by.

Seven o'clock the moon comes out
with the sleek girls in angora and leather
beside the pretty boys in their white jeans—
legs arced from the curb.

When the gardener closes the iron gates
the cats arrive, their furred backs
of smoke, ginger and calico,
tails snapping as they whip around the cemetery
dozens more on every headstone.

Darkness and the cars already begin to slow
and the gawkers lean over balconies,
the bars begin to smoke
and oh, the glory of,
the cops slouched waiting
because what could go wrong
will, soon enough.

THE BRIDE OF BAY

Finally, that first cracking day of spring.
A full-time job and payday
and tomorrow, a haircut and some clothes,
almost bourgeois.

Heading downtown
in my favourite old sweater
to find the first vendor
who sprongs his umbrella
like a curbside crocus
in a town where spring
is a roasted hot dog right from the cart
with extra onion and hot mustard on poppyseed.

Too early for the Blue Jays, I settle to consider
the sad ornithological order
in front of old city hall.
Wrens waggle their pert bums
as they nip off crumbs of bun, flinging them backwards
over their heads, those showoffs,
until the pigeons bump them
and then the gulls squatter in
and a mad-haired panhandler flaps them all away
as he commands the fountains to rise and fall
as coins are thrown in a box at his feet.

And the wind makes kites out of everything
and newspapers ride the updraft on Bay Street
wrapping themselves like obscene dogs
around businessmen's legs.
No more perfect use for the *Globe* than this.

And me warming in the pale sun
and the benches around the fountain
filled with the like-minded, warming their hands around
steaming cups.
Sure, there'll be another snowstorm,
but in two weeks the Jays open
and it's finally spring in Upper Canada.

Which is just fine
until I drop my keys in the trashbasket
along with my napkin.
With the help of gravity they are on the bottom.
The basket is very full of things
neither I nor anyone wants
except for, of course, my keys.
And it is, as I said, windy.
So I find a wire used to bundle newspaper
and begin to fish
somewhat earlier than I'd planned.

Soon I've sent a string
of garbage windward on Bay
hooking only a Coke can and a pair of panty house,
wondering how she did that in front of city hall.

I'm considering climbing in
when I realize I have an audience:
the wrens and their lurid bird giggles
while odder birds move in for a handout.
Decent people stare and now I'm head bird
in a flock that includes my friend
who circles me in glee,
flapping his arms.

Finally, I hook them, slightly mustardy
and I have to say—but deeply relished.
And as I turn windblown, a lot sheepish
and tattered, one of the decent folk,
a woman with good perfume, one of those
whose gloves guard the collection plate at church,
presses a ten into my hand
and before hurrying off says:
"Son, buy yourself a nice meal."

And I walk fast down Queen
that ten burning my hand
hotter than all the money I've ever made
and the bum chasing me
takes it gladly and shreds it,
stands with expensive confetti in his hair
at the corner of Business and Queen
grinning like a bride.

WHAT I KNOW ABOUT GERALD

That Gerry, the name the others called him,
was too joyful for his dignity.
That he was quiet and given to days of rage
when everything was dark.

That he was the only student
who ever told me I was wise
the day we talked about sprits
and how the earth is a holy mother.
That he was grey and moustached,
older than all the others.
That his fierceness was a necessary force to live by.

That he kept trying when the others failed.
That he was an Ojibwa from somewhere north of here,
from a school run by the priests.
That the things they did were unspeakable.
That he ran away and never returned.

That when I called the counsellor back,
all I had was scraps.
That she told me he was a roomer
in a place where no one knew him.
That he had a sister no one could find.
That he had tried twice before.

That he left a small bundle of possessions
and nowhere to send them.
That when he went down to Scarborough Bluffs
the spirit welcomed him.
That the waters of Lake Ontario consumed him.

That whatever wisdom I have is not enough.
That his grey eyes follow me as I watch my classes
for the watery arms that took him.

WHAT MY STUDENTS TEACH ME

Federico
tells me it's too cold here
but some choice.
You go out one morning,
the car hood's open a little;
three sticks of dynamite
and this is the third time.
In Salvador you take the hint:
you leave.

Ginny Fung
writes of the love
of her and her husband.
The first English she learned
was curses.
Those faces
she could read
in any language.

Cyrous
on the most profound moment of his life
writes a vague tribute
to world harmony and brotherhood.
When I question it,
he says,
I am a Baha'i from Iran.
This is for my friends,
not wanting me to seem foolish.
I nod dumbly as he explains
he was made to watch
as the blades fell
and their heads dropped in the street.

Leong Hiu
who now signs her name Lisa
has not seen her brother
since the night
the pirates boarded in the China Sea,
tells me she likes the winter here
because when she wakes
all the white stars are lying on the ground.

Shatha
tells the class
*I am visiting my mother after work
babysitting my sister's children
when the sirens went.
We hid under the table
covering my nieces with our bodies—
as the bombs fell the teapot shattered.
Everything crashing, it seemed forever.
You were watching that night
on your televisions: Desert Storm.*

Dan
says it began in April.
*Two million of us sir,
in the Square, I was so proud to be Chinese.
I was a reporter
when the official came into the office
and said, no more stories!
I was so angry I quit.
When the tanks came in June
—we ran, hearing the screams,
too scared to look back.
Now I can no longer write, I study computers*

Fardad
speaks of a trip to the front with his friend
who asked to drive.
We stopped for water.
I was gone a minute.
When I came out,
a missile—there was nothing left.
At the court martial, his mother screamed at me,
I should have been in his place.

And me,
what do I know.
I am a man on the beach
where the boats come in.

LETTERS HOME

IT'S BEEN SAID

"...you had to be in love with a woman to have a basis for friendship."
                          Ernest Hemingway, *Fiesta*

but how
we lived
on wind
wild salads
and dandelion wine
later walking into
the roman candle
of city lights
it was new then
magic of april kites
rainy days
when the wind whipped
trees into
emerald shimmers
and you danced me
in your wily ways
when i tried to remember
the almost perfect poem
exact lines since
forgotten
of a Spartan boy
bearing silently
the hungry fox
beneath his cloak
he dared not speak
cry out
i seldom did and often

too late
but there were a few
who loved you
for reasons the others hated
you daring
the things we whispered
instead
sailing kites
and singing sweet thunder
in the rain

LILACS

They were not
those mauve and lavender-scented
that suckered
around the window of my parents' bedroom
on the prairies.
Growing everywhere
those dry clustered pods
warning like rattlesnakes
in the wind.
More seed than flower.

Ours were the light and Japanese lilacs
that bloomed
at the window
of the first place we rented,
a basement room.
It was a summer of firsts
so we thought.

We had no vases
but the bedroom was filled
with jars of lilacs,
leaves growing underwater,
green fish, white moons.
And the scent that now belongs to light.

The taste of sage
on your neck.
Lilacs and footprints
in the hot bare dust,
all that's left.

One summer,
the old waft of light,
enough to remember
too much to desire.

PICKING APPLES

Not Northern Spies,
nor Granny Smiths. Yours
Plump Russets
rouged and weighty.
Or whatever.

When I learned to pick apples, two-handed
in the Niagara orchards,
weighing them in my palms,
the old orchardman showed me.
Letting gravity do its trick.
Lifting them away.

Their ripe and wondrous falling.
Their stems curled, a small leaf
fluttering like a sprouted wing.
Lowering them into the canvas
cradled on his chest.

And I had no idea then
he was talking about you,
or about love.

WHY THE FIELDS LIE FALLOW

True, there will be the usual crops:
corn, gourds, and blossoms in the orchard.

But the man is gone.
His wife remains in the new house
at the end of the orchard, the retirement home.

She watches the new couple
who bought the fields, the barn
and everything that came with them
the house where her children were born.

She sees in them all the photographs of the past.
She will find herself waking,
never in time quite reaching them.

She will reach out and touch what is real,
the cold heads of cabbages,
snapping fingers of beans.

Birds trail the harrow
as they have always done
and with mechanical twists make worms disappear
from the furrows of tawny earth.

Later she will sort their possessions
and pile them in a pyre on the hillside
where they used to burn the prunings
from the orchard, her and her other.

When the wind bangs the door on its hinges at noon,
she will catch herself
turning in that familiar way.

For a time her daughters will come home weekends,
take her hands in those moments
when she no longer remembers she is strong.
That it was her he looked to.

But soon she is alone again
with the silence, only the sounds of apple boughs
rapping on the house.

At dusk the dog will follow her
to the hillside under the black walnut tree
near the son who could have taken this from her.
She will remember how they buried him
and later all the children's pets,
the ceremony and the small crosses
overlooking the grassy slopes
that roll down to the river.

One day she will return
one furrow, wider and darker, open before her.
The arms of her husband and her children
will beckon her.

LETTERS HOME

Tonight, firesmoke
in that mountainous chute
where weather passes
from the coast to the prairies.

2000 miles and summer between us.
Here in my past
on the old rivers of liquid ice
where bank swallows still puff
from those clay 0's
above the floodline.
Landslides of scree and timber.
Violet loosestrife, and mullen
golden in the ditches.

Summerflowers bee-laden,
names I knew.
Alpine ponies in the high meadows.
Twenty years, still high over the Bow,
pastel balloons with wicker gondolas
swinging small as children's toys.
All things lovely,
out of reach.

While east of here, my present
and longing for
trains shunting under your curtainless window.
White linen tables of the café,
wine and shadows, couples
under the linden tree.
Hot bubbles of jazz
from the sax man on Bloor.

Smoke of the chestnut vendor's cart;
sleek men and women stepping out.
And your daughter asleep in the clouds
you painted in her bedroom
above the flower carts and perfect
balancing pyramids of oranges.
Lights on the Gardiner,
none of them bringing you.

There you lie,
mysterious, unreachable.
Your letters and your silk
across my thigh.
How the flesh
is both torn and caressed.

Everywhere this haze
while the aspens hush and crack
all night in the dry wind.

TIDAL BELLS

Awash, rising from you
like a grouty sea lion,
my whiskers askew with kelp.
In my hair and yours, sea grit,
our fingers salt rimed and foamed.

Shells in the slow tumble
from the westward current.
The spill of liquid sand,
whiffs of us.

Like those bright glass bulbs
loosened from the Japanese fishing nets.
Those clapperless tidal bells
tinking in the upcurl of waves,
lapping, just lapping like our tongues.

NERUDA IN THE KITCHEN

Your low-backed dress,
black-seamed stockings.
Your red hair.
No saint, you'd have preferred priesthood;
nuns always hidden away somewhere
and angels are dull.

That serene head staring towards me,
my eyes prisms of water
in which each ringlet of hair
becomes a strand in a wig of snakes,
each with the head of a man.
Nothing evil there,
simply all possibilities of belief.

Even when you stand still
things begin to happen.
In your kitchen, reading Neruda,
a mango in the other hand,
as if you'd forgotten which would be dinner.
The South Americans, you say, Marquez,
the others, not fantastical but Catholic,
straight from the *Lives of the Saints*.

Your blue gown flutters
as if risen from the ocean floor,
over your shoulder a shawl of beach.
In the room where poetry is made,
the words spread like peacocks
under the jacaranda trees.
Lizards slip from your fingers
into pools of low blue flames.

The mango still in the other hand,
you close the book
and as you split the green skin,
twelve parrots scramble for the window,
bolts of red and blue,
and you spill backwards into the night sky,
wave-rippled after them.
And me, I'm gripping an empty window-frame,
stunned but believing.

Santa Maria, saints are everywhere.

SLOW TRAIN HOME

We take our grief
from the new city to the old;
Montreal, St. Denis,
a carriage up cobbled hills.
Too soon yet for the boulevard cafés
but so little it takes to warm us.

Café au lait in hot bowls
steaming in our faces.
Notre Dame, a thousand candles
reeking of piety
under the statues of women martyrs
carved of old pine.

Rocking us homeward
shunted on to and off the main line
waiting out the long freights.
Your eager arms, ardent kisses.
Your body breaking open
and I'm gaping into it,
where that child was
we made one day at dawn.

Our bodies pressing, the train below
shaking us now
and the child somehow not dead
but passed back into us
where we warm it in our arms.

The slow train home,
starwash, rods of lupine frosty
by the stacked ties.
Leftover moon on the tables of the club car.
Others all sleeping.

We make love there
not out of daring but because we must.
The need to smash the body
back into molecules,
mesh with the stippled grasses
and muddied fields.

And dawn, the first green rain.
Innumerable moons implode in the window
with soft gasps of light.
Moving us from the old
into the new.
This terror
and all the cold new air.

LIGHT OVER MORNING

The third floor of a flat
on Tyndell Avenue
after the final streetcar trundles in,
she rises like a blind sleepwalker
to sit naked at the piano.
Ovoids of white buttocks on the cool bench,
the slope of her shoulders,
soft works of light.
Her fingers roll deftly on the keys
while the neighbours below dream melodically.

Her man sleeps
somewhere across the city.
An old story, a woman;
he left at Christmas time.

But consider her and the half-light
over the face, the elegant curve of her hair.
The way the music rises like drowsy love.
On the piano a conch shell
curled like a large pink ear.
And the light like a mist
waist-deep through the room.

And somewhere else, say Palestine
or a dozen other places,
in the same light
one man stalks another,
while her incendiary notes remain
pressed beneath fingertips.

But unlike those others
dying for scrubland, a village,
one God or Another,
this man, the lover
if he has yet lived
has done nothing to earn his death.
And I tell you,
he or any of us
does not deserve such music.

PREPARATIONS

This dry heave, the heart.
You prepare yourself
for that day years hence
when somewhere in the eye
the woman you loved at thirty-two,
but wanted at sixteen,
still there.

Her face in a certain fall light, pale
and the string loosened
on the spill of her breasts,
wonderful eyes insistent,
her cries, hair wispy on her neck;
all this, the difficult leaving.

The heart when dropped from a great height
has no wings.
A dumb bloody bag
that beats of its own accord.

And love never what you wish
but what you are doing now.
The rains of February diminish the snowbanks;
twisted coke cans, a single black glove,
newspapers on the stubs of the aster.
Under the loveseat a tortoise-shell comb.

Preparations begin.
Your eyes in your hands.
All the photographs upturned,
the stench of her everywhere,
sweet as leaves,
perfume and death.

THE ONES WITHOUT LOVERS

Saturday night in the Mars Diner
Facing the street, eating her toasted sandwich,
Her pie, reading her book.

The ones with lovers laugh without regard,
For those who are alone, but not lonely, so they say
The soft truths the solitary heart speaks, if at all.

Above the street, some play Scrabble on boards
Or screens glowing across the earth.
While others who are alone but not lonely.
Read books like this one
About reading about reading about themselves
And don't recognize each other on the street
Avert their eyes in panic; they know they know.

From the houses, too loud cries of birds,
And Hitchcock's droll droning,
Oldies over and over like a malady.
The alone but not lonely order
From the phonebook or the web
Someone, like pizza, like Chinoise, they say in M'real,
And pace the parquet, their feet kissing the floor
In expectation of exultation.

And their hands thrum briefly
Like Hitchcock's Birds,
Wings of madness alight
As all the lovers they've known, lost and imagined
Brush their eyelids with singed lips.

And the ones without lovers with children
Know they must let them go someday.
For now, thank themselves for their wisdom
As they wait for the door to close one last time.
It will always be too soon.

The alone and the lonely are not dancing tonight
But waving across the sky at each other.
Above the laughter, the frenzy of perfumed wrists
While the solitary diner reads the impossible poetry of
Neruda
Carnivorous for a bite of ear, neck, of lip.
And the Birds cacophonous
With that beat the heart has
in the dream it dares not make.

SARDINIA
(AS TOLD BY MARGARET)

Ours was a Cold War love.
Stationed on the Pine Tree,
second defence to the DEW Line,
south of Saskatoon in the grassy hills,
a stretch of radar domes,
like igloos across the near north.

We lived in the officers' compound,
I went back there once, just to see.
Nothing left now but loops of asphalt
where the trailers butted into the hillsides.

My husband in those long Saskatchewan nights,
told of Sardinia, his first posting.
And those Mediterranean girls
with their darker skin. Names he called out
as he reached for me in his sleep.

And we played cards:
kitchens and living rooms full of smoke.
With other couples, always officers and their wives,
none of us unmatched, as we bowled in the two lane alley
next to the officers' mess.
All the codes of dress and decorum.
And I never suspected a thing.

Worked down in the county office typing.
While he took swing shifts in the radio tower,
that's now a shell on the hill, the white dome gone.
Eavesdropping on the talk of Soviet pilots
and our own in the high Arctic.
A man who'd read Chekhov in the Russian.

The day the cat smelled of perfume
it all came together
as it fell apart.
When her husband mentioned to her
mine had requested a transfer to Sardinia,
and she broke down, told him everything.

And my husband, trained in code
and cyphers, the man I thought I knew, stayed silent.
All those secret glances, the double entendres he loved
—the pokerface.

All the reasons she told me later, I've forgotten,
but not her red eyes, the stain of my slap spreading on her cheek,
and I hugged her like a sister,
my nose in that damned perfume of hers.

MANTA RAY

In Kensington Market
between the greengrocer's
truck, bottomed out
with over-ripe pineapples
and the cheeseman's
bagel-steamed front,
the fishmonger's boy
carries it
arm's-length from his chest
stacked onto milk crates
while a crowd gathers.

An odd cross between a shark
and homeplate,
the supple razor of its tail
coiled in broken mangoes.
A hacksaw grin
that widens as rigor mortis sets in
and the grey skin buckles and dries.
The eyes pale sunken figs
that the wasps warm to
where someone has inserted—
one bent forward,
another tilted outward
—red horns of pimento.

Oh love,
to think once I saw you
feathered and vain.
How you loved a crowd,
the flash of your teeth.
No bird
but second cousin to a shark.

WHEN WE WERE LOVERS

I wanted to be Italian
to change my name to Di Cicco
or Pavese; I learned
to drink cappuccino,
acquired a taste for pesto,
women in Florentine leathers,
chic hats and seamed stockings
in the Café Roma.
None of this was difficult.

And my Jamaican friend
looks amused when I explain
how the Scots and the Irish hate the English
—and the English hate everyone else—
all the shades of white.
He thought we all looked the same.

My Anglo friends want to be Italian too.
When all we have
is the man in the Irish Spring commercial
in a tweed cap
and of course, Prime Minister Muldoon.

But now I'm confused
if it was you or the romance
of olive trees and a Mediterranean skin
always darker than mine,
a language more capable of rage.

Mine is the lost tongue,
of my uncles, their bagpipes,
the beat of a battle hymn
four hundred years ago.

But how wrong I was
for each day my blood darkens
with new rage for this.
And the only word I remember now
in Italian
is ciao.

DEATH OF THE BLACK CAT

The grey cat peers from the night table and whines
so unlike him, urgent, and when I rise to feed him,
the silver tabby around my ankles, I find the black cat
lying on his side before the bedroom door;
my hand goes to his ribs, the chest no longer rises,
the body is warm, the tail supple between my fingers.
He's died in mid-stride, returning from the birds feeding
at the front window at dawn, cat television in our house,
coming back to my wife's pillow, his heart likely,
after months of death watch; the vet warned us
he won't come back easily next time,
he has a heart murmur. This strange, small creature
with a shortened tail, appeared at our door
on a winter's day ten years ago; and after months
of feeding him, on the occasion of my birthday,
we let him in and he never left,
pleased with a warm place and food, on my wife's
pillow at night, on my cap or coat, sometimes
even on my keys. A lost cat has found us
on the trail for three thousand years to the Highland crofts
from the savannas and the fires, feeding with us
and following. The tabby and the grey watch
as I stroke him and gasp, "Oh no". My wife
suddenly awake, begins to sob, and from the next room
my old friend, Billy, tall and grizzened,
a farmer now, goes with me, as the sun comes up,
the black cat wrapped in a towel with a unicorn on it,
burying superstition and myth in the same grave.
I hold him in a sling, his head and tail
still drooping, but his eyes don't answer me.
And I lie him on the grass in a grove of black cedars

that seems always to have been waiting for this,
where my wife's family buried generations of dogs,
her pet duck and someone's pony.
A scene somewhat Faulknerian in Southern Ontario.
As I sharpen my spade with a file, Billy watches
and my wife cradles the black cat and softly wails.
We are childless, and these animals are more
than children, perfect and silent,
as children never should be. I cut the sod
and square the hole, bevelling the sides,
a perfect small grave. My wife later asks me
how did you know to do it, and I can't explain.
Even the gravediggers I worked amongst
in Niagara drove backhoes;
perhaps it's an earlier memory than my own
I tell her. I was a gardener not a gravedigger,
planting never burying, work always
begun in hope not despair. Billy stops me,
I think it's deep enough, he says, as if
I've been digging for something bigger all my life.
Watching his father, the Dutch gardener,
him seven years gone now—so much lies behind us—
both of us still learning from him,
watching, though the Ogden boys we once were,
growing up beside the rail yards,
never called it a spade, always a shovel.
All I'm sure of now is the earth
between the hard metal and my hands,
carefully mounding it beside the small deep hole;
everything deserves this grace. My wife
hands him to me, and I kiss the black fellow's snout
before I lower him, and she tosses in a stuffed mouse
he loved—what's good enough for the pharaohs
is good enough for the black cat. No tears

are shed in front of Billy, though we'd both understand.
When it's done, I tamp the earth gently,
replace the sod and for weeks afterwards,
everywhere in the shadows, I see the black cat
and wait for him to come out. My wife
says nothing; we are past the time of children
but not the time of desire or noticing,
or the need to love something both smaller
and greater than ourselves,
to pass on the lives we've lived, or the love.
My friends say about their children,
if they could do it again, they wouldn't—
the words of the blessed. When you have had love,
it's easy to say, we could have done without.
But a month after we buried the black cat,
the grave is level and only an outline of gravel left
where the grass is slow to grow
between the black cedars; I come home from travelling
tired, and, at 2:00 a.m. my wife wakes me;
I'm wheezing like a cow and my breath stops.
We drive to Emergency, humid air
in the windows of the truck, our town quiet,
and I lie for a long time, listening
to the woman in the next bed, crying,
whose transplant has failed, to the children in pain,
and I'm grateful for only this.
The doctor orders x-rays
and I'm wheeled through the darkened halls,
the hazy breeze lifting my gown, the automatic doors
opening one after another. This is
a small town; I will see her tomorrow
at the market or Tim Hortons. I apologize to the sleepy
radiologist, for getting her up. She laughs
and lifts my arms around the x-ray, and I hug

the machine that stares into my heart.
It's nothing I tell my wife, before I drift,
intravenous in my arm; we'll be fine.
Until I'm wakened by her hand on my shoulder, and
the doctor shows me the outline of my heart, the fluid,
enlarged, failure the only word I hear. My father and I
longest ticking of all those damn Scots hearts—
no uncles or grandfathers in my family.
There is the banality of evil and the ordinariness of death.
He sends me home to wait for the tests
and a visit with my own doctor. I am not afraid,
this is how it happens to most of us, one day
we go and they tell us it's time.
The details suddenly don't matter anymore.
I sit up, watch the sun rise over the house
the black cedars full of birds, as they were last winter,
thousands warming the air with their wings;
they scrabble in the eaves, swinging down
to the feeders, jays, grackles, in the trees, crows,
on the roof mourning doves. I sleep on the couch
where the black cat did, watching
the sparrows in the dogwood, and the goldfinches.
Later I go to my desk, find the form the lawyer gave me
years ago for a will, a form I'd scoffed at, too soon,
and I find my pen, write instructions for the work
that needs to be done, notes for the book
I've nearly finished, but I've no regrets.
For twelve hours I wait, unable to sleep, but not awake,
walking in the yard I've cleared of dead trees,
opening it to the sky, like the prairies of my youth.
I'm not old, only no longer young, and I'm grateful
for the bushes I've planted, weigela and ferns,
Nootka cedar, purple hazel and the new maples,
the green lope of the lawn towards the swans and the river.

Always I've wanted land I could die on,
though I know unlike the black cat
I won't be buried here.
And I'm grateful for these hours
until the doctor calls. There's been a mistake,
something about the x-ray and the intern's inexperience,
a friend he apologizes for; I had supper with him
the other night. The way it is in small towns.
I thank him. Later, my wife is angry,
but I'm grateful for both the news
and the rehearsal, I tell her,
never wasting anything in my life,
except time, knowing now that I have days, months,
or maybe years, but not forever; one day
this is how it will be and it's a shame
to waste a death or a life—
and that I would do it all again.

COMING HOME FROM HOME

JOHN/JOHN

the Bighorn Stoneys
called him John-John
knew something we didn't
there was always two of him
the reality, five seven
steel pins in both knees
two fingers missing
hearing aid in one ear
like Indians
wore his scars on the outside
but i'm not interested in the facts
we're dealing with legend here
the other, his best story
himself, in the telling

this is my language
his, crow speak
back country lumber camps
Cree song and radio talk

if he wasn't first
he was last
last ranger in the Forest Service
to use dog teams
tells of the day on the ice
of the Upper Saskatchewan
on the way to the Dolomite
dogs caught whiff of wild horse
took six miles to stop 'em
not a bad place to camp anyway
named it

(in a new district
you named everything
helped you know where you were)
Wildhorse Creek

family never sure
of him or the story
like the dog sled
ordered from H.B.C. Winnipeg
when it arrives
he measures, blueprints
sends it back unused
improvises with axehandles
and sleigh parts
this way he invented himself

on the barn wall, strange tools
hoof trimmers, adzes, scythes
come-alongs, slings, pack pumps
hot coals and horseshoe metal
John cranking the bellows
watches the sky
remembering similar coals
in the rock high above Pinto Lake
no soil no water
just dry sacks, shovels
stamping feet all night
watching cinders drift
onto the crowns of dry timber
in the valley below
no accident his curses
were words of prayer

did he make the other
the taller one
out of loneliness, of whimsy
one would tell the joke
the other sat back
were there two
or were there two times
twice as many
that makes him four
needed all the help
you could get

soft talking Cree
in a back country cook tent
up the Bighorn River
with Walking Buffalo
last of another kind
grey braids, in white doeskin
with John trading
in the language of cougar
hurrying birds, squirrel warnings
of early winter and spring flood

in the corral on horseback
with a string of packponies
packboxes diamond-hitched
carbine under saddlebag
Forest Service khaki
you could almost believe again
in uniforms, easier times

picking berries near dark
from the house his wife watches
John on one end of the bush
on the other, bear
moving towards each other unaware
Kathy runs out with the .303
bear heads for the river
John over the woodpile
he'll tell you he wasn't sure
who she was gonna shoot

the tale whispered
the telling one
of his favourite son show stayed home
(the others left
the living, with legend, hard)
let his father's colt into muskeg
remembering the temper
the snakeskin whip
hung at the back door by the rifles
took a rifle instead, two cartridges
one for the drowning horse
the other for himself

my brother in forestry camp
ten years later, hears the story
from outfitters and up-river trappers
the story retelling itself
around fires, in bar rooms
time he lost two fingers
off his right hand
drove the forestry truck
standard steering, manual shift
90 miles over washboard roads

into Rocky Mountain House
nurse found him out cold
on the front steps of the hospital
when he left told the doctor
he'd wanted the dead fingers
never threw anything away in the bush

at 75 retired to town
with five greenhouses
fifteen dogs and a horse
no one can ride
Stoneys come a hundred fifty miles
to talk, buy his flowers
he knows what they want
not live ones that die
and with them the spirit
but dried ones like those
that stand all winter
above the snow
like John

SOURCES

Playing on a Y of willow
or iron rebar or bent coathanger,
whether it's a cup of water
or a river
it's always the same tensile tune
pitched high in his ears.

Because, he told me
the water dowser's strung
like a gut
between the air
and the secret rivers below.

He tells of his mother's torment:
sleepless for years
and when he dowsed her bedroom
below her pillow
rushed an ancient and subterranean river
that near yanked the bar
from his hands.

All those years the family laughed at her
convinced that the brain
knows better than her nocturnal ear,
that same ear he'd been god-given.

THE SCOTTISH GRANDMOTHERS

And the long ago love of them,
stomping from the bus stop
with their Hudson's Bay shopping bags
of cinnamon buns. Their little houses
smelling of broth and camphor.

Their calfskin Bibles
and fishing tackle
in the top of the hall closet,
the only opulence in their dour lives,
root beer fermenting from things
gathered on the prairie—an old world recipe
that exploded once or twice, glass in everyone's
shoes, among the pious names of the prophets
passed from Bible to children, the psalms
and epiphanies slightly scented
of root beer.

Those small defiant women
whose generosity came from austerity,
one of them rolling her smokes,
"Hell, cheap? We were poor.
And your Aunt Maggie wrote:
Cold here—don't come.
I did anyway."

And whatever gifts given them at Christmas
always returned to the sender at birthdays
or other Christmases.
Not a white glove among them,
their chin hairs and eyebrows
never tweezed until the undertaker got them.
Their stories come back in mine

—all the long lines of the Scottish grandmothers
bearing teaboxes of shortbread
over legendary hills of gorse and heather,
the wind scented always
of cinnamon and root beer.

THE NIGHT YOU DIED

You passed through one last time
and though I've seen ghosts all my life
I almost didn't believe it,
thought it memory's way
of keeping the present for the future
as poetry is the heart's reckoning with reason.

But the room cooled suddenly
and your presence woke me—
you were on your way home, somewhere
and it was urgent
that you pass through one more time,
that I see you.

Though I still didn't completely believe—
but you had one last thing to show me.
Later, I lay awake thinking of the time
I dared Charlie I could find water
—it's bullshit, I said,
hoping it would fail,
though I knew of electrical fields
between water and the body.
I've studied too much science
to completely disbelieve.

We found a willow fork,
though he told me a crowbar
would work just as well,
and we found water
and I became a sceptical disbeliever.

And when you passed through
I wanted to believe this was memory
dealing with itself,
not that tug
between the arms and body of the dowser,
the water and clay.

Pliant as willow, taut
as the line between
the trout we never caught
and the heart that hoped we would,
a force field pulling me back into the earth
between belief and disdain,
holy terror and exaltation.

It had to be you
and when I slept finally
my dreams were trout streams
leaping with light.

CHASING THE TRAIN

Between Toronto and Stratford
on the C.N.'s main line, west of Guelph
where Scottish stonemasons' work lines the track
the country opens up green and stony
and farmers are named Glendinning.

You'll see a border collie, a legless roundabout blur
of black and white,
a solitary Highlander in a sheepless pasture,
chasing the train a full quarter mile
flat-out along the fence.

So strong the urge to work, that twice
each day, she's after the gleaming silver Superliner
hurtling to and from Chicago,
windows full of tourists expecting sheep.

And I'm betting one day, she'll break past
the fences, seize the train by its tail.
Whatever would she do
with eight double-decked silver coloured sheep
if she caught them? But that's quibbling,
for a working dog in a pasture without sheep,
who's been bred for centuries,
she's not wondering at all.

Just bound determined she's going to,
one of these days,
even as she stops at the fence.
Next time, her eyes and tilted tongue say,
as she lets us go, barrelling home.

THE TOMB AT DUNN

I found him that day I walked down Eighth Avenue,
a month after my grandmother's funeral,
past the Glenbow, and remembered in her time
it was called Stephen Avenue
when the sandstone buildings
and the gaslights ranged to the prairies.

Begg, I asked the archivist,
her eyes averted. Everyone claims family here.
Nothing left I thought,of the loquacious family
my great-great grandfather
who wrote *A History of British Columbia.*

But she came back, six boxes of letters,
two hundred items of clothing and tools from the ranch,
His poetry and maps, photographs and diaries:
"I've left my native land forever.
I fear I shall not see her again."

His handwriting changed with the voyage
and after weeks of seasickness:
"I am overjoyed to see
the cliffs of Quebec City, my new home."

His notes on the pictures,
guide me now to the northeast coast,
above the 68th parallel, Finland and Norway over there.

Coming home to Caithness, where in the pubs
Canada's still a distant dream of wilderness and Indians,
one hundred and sixty years
after my great-great grandfather sought it
and I've followed him back across the sea.

On the road to John O'Groats and the Orkneys,
we find the village of Watten and the Brown Trout
where the farmers drink.
Our last night before we go home to Canada,
a name we now hear as adventure.

"Begg," one local says, "means small in Gaelic."
"And square," another snorts, "low to the land."
"And hairy," a shaggy one nods.
They laugh, stout furry men themselves, a Scottish gale
whines outside, everything low in this treeless green north.

"Has anyone know of their croft?"
our waitress asks, and the pub begins reminiscing
about everyone else, revelling in the past.
"I remember them," a farmer in gumboots says.
"No, Colin Geddes, have ya' not got ears.
It's Begg, not Bate." someone argues.

Another waitress appears at our table,
and the whole pub has forgotten us in their stories.
"The place you're seekin' is on my farm,
but you'll not want to be goin' there
on a night like tonight."

But the sun sets here at eleven and there's
two more hours of northern light, so we go
to a barley field up the road
rimmed with gorse and broom,
wind-flattened and rain-bent,
New World gortex barely helps
as the rain comes up and around, lifting our hoods.
"You can't miss it," she'd said,

"And we're almost there," I say to my wife,
my father's words every time we got lost.
But in this light, every glen
resembles the one we want,
and every grove is tall to a stranger,
until we find the low stone fence,
built of boulders from the nearby sea,
here in the stony and green north
where great sheets of shale
hang like plywood along the pastures.

An iron stile creaks near the empty hole
the ancient tomb has tumbled in.
Branches whip from the low trees,
clustered near the stonepiles of crofts,
all that is left, shadows in the rain.
A good place for a horror movie, I say to the wind,
and then my wife screams.
She touched a tombstone
alive with slugs.

But we've come this far, back across the ocean,
by luck and a memory older than mine,
finding the clues my grandmother left
her father and his and the ones before him.
The clouds have blocked
the setting sun and we are alone with the dead.

Over here, she shouts, I've found them.
On my knees, I scrape the stones:
William Begg, Tacksman, born 1759. Mary Begg born 1763.
Between them an oak sapling sprouts.

I prune the tree with my knife, cut away
the moss, my nails clogged with Scottish mud.
I know this is the last time
anyone will come from North America
and the land will take back the stones
as it has the Tomb at Dunn, as it has them.

For now, I honour my family with my hands
cutting away the grass
and the earth that has begun its work.
And since there are no parish clark's records,
their words end here.

There's nothing more than the clues of our names,
and the walking down cobblestone streets
of Wick and watching the cannon in Stromness harbour
that hailed the Hudson's Bay boats leaving for the new world.
This was the harbour he sailed from.

Everywhere I see faces like my own
and in Paisley as we take an airport bus
a woman smiles. Later, as the plane lifts
over Glasgow, when it's safe, I know
it's my grandmother's face
and I'm not the first to lose tears over the Atlantic
leaving those streets, those faces of family.

I went to find myself and instead got lost:
returning with a Flemish name, Bruce,
people of the brush,
given to a Scottish hero
and a name favoured by the English nobility
—for their dogs.

Mine a mongrel mix of Nordic and Celtic blood,
from Tuscany and Turkey
and when one of my students mistakes me for a Jew,
I love the holy confusion of the New World
and know why I've always loved the Russian poets
who knew all this.

And I go one more time to the Glenbow,
where the curator holds up the kilt
and the jacket. Like me, my great-great grandfather
a small man with tiny feet.
I'm driven to foolishness and dreams,
poetry and wandering,
and the certainty I sought once
now replaced with the knowing
we are the parts of history,
not always the ones we wish.

HOMEWORDS

Your father turned back
by Riel's men at Pembina in 1869,
told of the Highland Clearances
impoverished plots of land,
subdivided between sons and sons of sons,
and then the English. Why he'd fled.

But you remembered what he said about those new plains,
the great humped buffalo, the savages,
Canaans he called them.
When you finished college in Guelph,
there was only one way to go. West.

These are the words that began the journey;
you kept them among the pictures of family.
Bills of lading for your cherished horses.

Dominion of Canada
Department of the Interior
               Ottawa 30th May, 1886

Dear Sir,

  I am instructed by the Minister of
the Interior to acknowledge the
receipt of your letter of the 29th
ultima that Robert
Anstruther Begg will be permitted
entry for the North East-quarter

of Section 12, Township 21,
Range 28, West of the Fourth
Meridian upon applying to
The Agent of Dominion Lands
at Calgary for that purpose
and upon payment to him
at the usual entry fee. As a
prior application to

> I have the honor to be,
> Sir,
> R. D. Douglas
> Assistant Secretary

Man of letters, my great-grandfather, boy who left home.
West before the railway, Missouri paddle wheelers,
by wagon, north from Fort Benton
with his horses to the confluence
of the Highwood and the Bow.
The buffalo were gone, 1879.

Nailing the corral fence, one day,
barred slats of light and the sudden shadow
a Blackfoot raiding party
in full warpaint, you wrote.

What's a boy to do.
Handful after handful of loose tea
tossed into the pot, you invited them in
sat on the floor, all of you drinking strong tea.

13 years later, Will Rogers' in your letters:
Dear Mama,
Norah and Dottie fine…but Sandy's colicky and…
You sign off:
A man's nothing but a great big grown-up old boy.
Regards to Papa, Bob.
p.s. Bean says hello

Vast tracts between ellipses.
College boy who fought the Dominion's
faraway bureaucrats,
ostracized by the locals,
you'd not break grazing land.
Already you knew the wind, benchland over the Bow
palomino grass that fed your horses
too dry for wheat.

They threatened to take the homestead
if you'd not plough. You stayed true to the land, the wind.

Two years ago, with your old map,
I find a NWMP track scratched
out on the Whoop-up Trail
and your first home a log hut
for stopovers on the way north to Fort Calgary,

No road still, so I wade the Highwood, the Bow
rushing past me.
I find the lush green place you chose.
Too young to know a flood plain
of a glacier fed river. They didn't teach that at Guelph.
You'd find out soon enough, water lifting the furniture.

We never lived anywhere in our family

more than ten years. You lasted 30 here.
For the children
you moved your family into town, but not yourself.

Began to wander then,
cattle-buying boy, you kept moving
west through the ranches of BC.

There's no ghosts here now on the Highwood
only the fresh skull of a calf, putrid meat
in its cavity that the wolves and crows
couldn't get before I boiled it white.

The name your father gave this place, Dunbow
after Dunn on the road to John O'Groats and Orkney
running off Macleod Trail on the old Fort Benton road.
Drove by hundreds of times.
Never gave a thought until I found your map.

All along the tableland,
the cattle companies still—
you were right college boy. Prime grazing land.
Those who broke it, lost it.
This place of rolling grassy dunes
blonde stalks bend in the wind
honour the home that is looking for you still.

COMING HOME FROM HOME

Eighteen years in exile—
gone from the Gaelic city of my birth
to the land that sent the men to hunt Riel.

Riel voted by his people
to the Parliament of Canada—
Riel the poet, the prophet—
who prayed to God
when Dumont had the bastards cornered.

Eighteen years still haunted by the ghost of the man
who stepped aside on the word of Macdonald
while Cartier went in Riel's stead.

And a few years later, needing votes
in the country of the Orangeman Scott,
Macdonald sent troops
after a man who trusted him.

(Riel elected three times to Parliament
by his people, went once, signed in and left
before the clerk spotted him.
But that night all Ottawa came to the public gallery.
Riel slipped away fearing for his life.)
A man who loved his country too much to stay away.

Riel of whom my great-great grandfather wrote home
to Emily in Orillia, October 31, 1869
from Pembina, Manitoba:
"My dear wife, I'm wrapped in
a buffalo robe, my fingers freezing

we have lost our horses and have been
wandering the prairies for weeks.
The road barricaded ten miles
from here by a hand of half breeds
led by a Jesuit. I'm afraid
we must turn back."

I'm torn for the land I've left,
and come to love the land that kept the bell from Batoche
until three years ago a truck with Saskatchewan plates
driven, some say, by the ghost of Dumont, stole it back
from the Legion Hall—gone forever
in the revenge of Batoche
and I tell you, I had nothing to do with it.

Living in the country of the Orangeman,
and the judge who sentenced him to hang,
I'm still shaken by the memory of Riel, a Catholic,
and how home is a dubious name
for what the heart can't have—
this land where my great-great grandfather's
son left school, to ride west before the railroad
and take up land at the confluence of the Bow and Highwood
—for services rendered in the Rebellion—
but he learned at Guelph and wrote the Dominion's men,
"grazing land", he'd not plow it
and to this day it's unbroken,
cattle companies along the Bow.

But the green Ontario boy couldn't know how
his lush meadow on the best trout stream
in the south-east was a flood plain,
this land that his father
from the stormy northeast of Scotland
where the Norsemen landed
named it after the town of his birth
and the river—Dunbow—
the need to name our place, each other,
this time, this year.

They left me no land
only this diseased Nordic light that blinds me now—
like them, I have wandered
and everywhere is home when home is nowhere
near anywhere anymore.
And the names keep changing—
mine Flemish for people of the brush,
theirs Gaelic for a small people.
Their Highland dancing shoes
fit my tiny feet.

Eighteen years in exile
in the land of the men who hanged Riel
and I move too easily among them
not safe from the memory
knowing that to name us and this place
is to fix us only for an instant
on a map we crossed and
crossed out again
and again.

Leaving the stones of the croft,
the Tomb at Dunn, the graveyard and its markers,
the fallow grass of the ranch and the rutted
cart tracks filled with runoff. And oh,
those letters, if we are lucky,
long after love's hushed
and the lovely letters of their names
keep us coming home from home.

TWO O'CLOCK CREEK

All that summer couldn't understand
in the morning as we drove through
dry boulder wash, the matter-of-fact sign nailed
on a creekside spruce:
   TWO O'CLOCK CREEK
—and no water anywhere.

Me twelve with Uncle John on patrol
in the forestry truck.
Him hungover and with that temper,
you didn't push the obvious.

But that sign taunted me.
As first ranger in the district
he named things factually like an explorer:
Abraham flats after a Stony chief.
The map men kept that one,
thinking it Biblical and it was, in a way.

But each afternoon, driving back, sure enough
at two o'clock, there was a creek
roaring cold under the wheels.

Finally, a week before school and the city, I asked,
a prairie boy baffled by the magic of water
appearing anywhere, and on time.
John smirks, swings the Ford
into the ditch and around,
a madman on his way to a holy place.

I hang on as we climb, boulders boil in the fenders.
Double-clutching down into first
onto a horsetrail, then straight up on foot,
a pika whistling at us. Beginning to wish
I hadn't asked about that sign.

Over the alpine meadows
a plateau where mountain sheep startle
at the two of us covered in dust.
He draws his pipe across the foot of a glacier
tipped from the distant sky, a white glory
scooped into the sunslope
in a sheltered cowl of rock.
John points to a green waterfall
spilling over the lip.

Here sky meets land
and water is hard as rock this high
and liquid ice to the tongue and our aching feet.
Where all the rivers begin,
the Whitegoat, the Bighorn
after the sheep behind us.
Headwaters of the upper Saskatchewan
I knew from schoolroom maps,
coursing down to Hudson Bay
with canoes full of *coureur de bois*.

Below us, blonde grass riffles on Kootenay Plains,
clouds jam the chute the weather comes through
where the Kootenay descended to barter the Cree.
Up here the wind howls cold.

And I saw how a few hours of daylight
warms the ice to a trickle that becomes a torrent
in the glacier's pit. The mystery of rivers
is that they come from somewhere
between earth and sky.
wrung by the sun from clouds and wind.

But when night comes, Two O'clock Creek sleeps,
the waterfall waits frozen, and all the years
since I learned how rivers are made,
this is the place I come to in my dreams
between the highest point of land and the sky,
so I can drink from the clouds.

RECURRING DREAMS ON A GARDEN

The garden
—always back to the garden.

And the Dutch gardeners of my dreams:
Billy's father tilling
his velvet loam spilled
against the brome-covered hills of Alberta.

Gleaming white rails of the fence,
a dyke against the drought.
Weeding the intruders:
prairie clover, portulaca, thistle.

Sometimes there is an arbour
dream-borrowed from my parents' yard
with its vines and swinging gate,
hanging on its single rasping hinge.

And then, last night, I am unable to move,
so I wave from this side of the dream.

Billy's father raises a glove,
affable, a man loving his garden,
thinking his way through the rows.

And only when I wake,
rested from its innocence,
do I know why the latch lay closed,
why I can't get there.

Him, seven years dead,
all that time preparing the earth to receive him,
now gone to the green heaven.

THE LAST DAYS OF KLEIN

There is death
and then there is the end
which begins before the other.
The body insists always on remaining
when even the eyes
already cloud with the ash
of what has been.

The gifted tongue
chides children and the dog.
Hands drum hollow
upon the desk.
Books proffer only dust.
The last will is folded in a drawer.
The green blotter is ordered
and visited like a grave.

EDEN ON FLAMINGO

In the sweet heat of summer,
the Ashkenazi girl squats
on her tanned haunches
in the garden's soft loam,
eating tomatoes spotted with last night's rain,
catching droplets with her tongue.

Her Sephardic toes remember the sand,
Canaan and the rocks.
Her dark tresses dangle
damp as she turns: Try one,
they're really good, she offers,
the white underside of her forearm
extended towards me,
sun on her bare shoulders,
skin that hints of olive groves.
The voice is Eve's.

And the tilt of her head,
lavender lush of her eyelids,
proud chin, petalled lips,
black faraway eyes, Mizrachi.
All the lost and haunted tribes.
But this is Thornhill, not Eden.

Wherever we wander,
history and love everywhere.
Summer's motorcycles whinge
on the freeway behind us.

And amongst the plants that follow us:
wild carrots, sprawling thyme and lemon balm,
the cupped ears of bellflowers
not pealing but listening.

*Ashkenazic, Sephardic and Mizrachi Jews are,
respectively, from Eastern Europe, Spain, Portugal,
North Africa and the Middle East.

Acknowledgements

The author is grateful to the editors and publishers of the following in which earlier versions of these poems appeared.

Anthologies:

Writing the Terrain, Alberta centenary anthology, University of Calgary Press. 2005. *Smaller than God: words of spiritual longing*, Black Moss Press, 2001. *Following the Plow: Recovering the Rural*, Black Moss Press, 2000. *2000% Cracked Wheat*, Coteau Press, 2000. *Line By Line, Poems and Drawings*, Ekstasis Editions, 1999. *A Rich Garland: Poems for A.M. Klein*, Vehicule Press, 1999. *The Summit Anthology*, Banff Centre Press, 1999. *90 Poets of the Nineties, An Anthology of American and Canadian Poetry*, Seminole Press, 1998. *In the Clear*, Thistledown Press, 1998. *What Is Already Known*, 20th Anniversary Celebration, Thistledown Press, 1995. *Paperwork*, Harbour, 1990. *Your Voice and Mine*, Holt Rinehart, 1987. *No Feather, No Ink*, Thistledown Press, 1985. *Dancing Visions, New Poets in Review*, Thistledown Press, 1985. *Glass Canyons: Calgary Writing*, NeWest Press, 1984. *New Voices, A Celebration of New Voices*, Mosaic Press, 1984. *Going For Coffee*, Harbour, 1981.

Journals

Canadian Forum, Dandelion, Event, Grain, Germination, NeWest Review, Poetry Canada Review, Rags, Repository, River King, Wascana Review, 3c Pulp, Waves, Wee Giant, Wot, Zymergy.

Radio

Several of these poems were broadcast nationally on CBC's Anthology program and others were broadcast regionally on Alberta Anthology and Daybreak Alberta.

I also wish to express my deep gratitude my dear friend, the late Sonja Skarstedt for her enthusiasm and support for this project. Many others over the years, have also lent their ears, to name just a few: Cynthia Chambers, Chris Faiers, Barry Dempster, Ken Dyba, Phil Hall, Robert Hilles, Charles Noble, Paddy O'Rourke, Ken Rivard, Glen Sorestad, and Richard Stevenson. Finally, I would like to thank Ron Smith and Randal Macnair for their continued belief in my work.

Photograph by Korby Banner

About the author

James Reaney in the London Free Press called Bruce Hunter one of the great chroniclers of Canada's working people and the "Hank Williams of Canadian literature". Wayson Choy wrote in Saturday Night: "Bruce Hunter writes with bold restraint and a poet's sensibility. His blue-collar characters walk the tight line of the common universe that includes us all."

Born in Calgary, Alberta, Bruce was deafened as an infant and is the oldest of seven children. He was raised in the shadow of the Canadian Pacific Railway's now decommissioned Ogden Shops. His father was a "tinbanger" or sheet metal worker. His mother was a homemaker, and later, an arts student and artist. Bruce's great-grandfather was one of Alberta's first ranchers.

After high school, Bruce worked variously as a labourer and equipment operator, before attending Malaspina College where he studied with Ron Smith who encouraged his writing. After completing a horticultural apprenticeship, Bruce worked for several years as a gardener in Alberta and in Southern Ontario.

While doing these jobs, he published poetry in several journals which led to a scholarship to the Banff School of Fine Arts where he studied with W.O. Mitchell, Irving Layton, Sid Marty and Eli Mandel, among others. At age 28, he attended York University where he studied film and literature, while taking writing courses from Don Coles, bp Nichol, and Miriam Waddington. He also drove a Zamboni in the university's ice rink to pay the rent. While at York, Bruce published his first full-length poetry collection, Benchmark, in 1982. It was broadcast nationally on CBC Radio's Anthology program and was one of the most widely reviewed books of poetry in Canada that year.

On graduation, he taught creative writing at York University and the Banff School of Fine Arts. He then joined Toronto's Seneca College in 1986, where he has been a professor of English and Liberal Studies since. He now teaches the poetry and spoken word workshops there.

For the past 30 years, Bruce has lived in various parts of southern Ontario including Stratford and Toronto. He now resides in Thornhill.